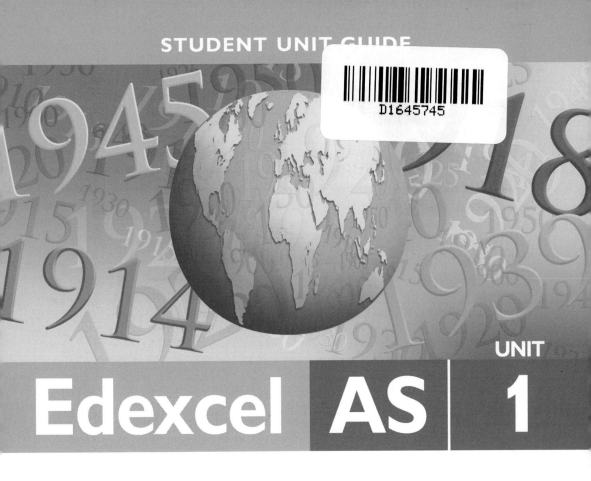

STUDENT UNIT GUIDE

D1645745

UNIT

Edexcel AS | 1

History

Russia in Revolution, 1881–1924:
From Autocracy to Dictatorship
(Option D3)

Derrick Murphy

Philip Allan Updates, an imprint of Hodder Education, an Hachette UK company, Market Place, Deddington, Oxfordshire OX15 0SE

Orders

Bookpoint Ltd, 130 Milton Park, Abingdon, Oxfordshire OX14 4SB
tel: 01235 827720
fax: 01235 400454
e-mail: uk.orders@bookpoint.co.uk
Lines are open 9.00 a.m.–5.00 p.m., Monday to Saturday, with a 24-hour message answering service. You can also order through the Philip Allan Updates website: www.philipallan.co.uk

© Philip Allan Updates 2009

ISBN 978-0-340-99043-8

First printed 2009
Impression number 5 4 3 2 1
Year 2014 2013 2012 2011 2010 2009

This guide has been written specifically to support students preparing for the Edexcel AS History Unit 1 examination. The content has been neither approved nor endorsed by Edexcel and remains the sole responsibility of the author.

Typeset by DC Graphic Design, Swanley Village, Kent
Printed by MPG Books, Bodmin

Hachette UK's policy is to use papers that are natural, renewable and recyclable products and made from wood grown in sustainable forests. The logging and manufacturing processes are expected to conform to the environmental regulations of the country of origin.

P01473

Contents

Introduction

■ ■ ■

Content Guidance

■ ■ ■

Questions and Answers

Introduction

About this unit

Unit 1 is worth 25% of the A-level course (50% of the AS). It requires knowledge of the topic and the ability to explain historical events and assess their significance in a wider context. There are no sources in the exam, so source skills are unnecessary.

Questions require you to provide clear information that directly answers the question. In addition, examiners are looking for detailed and precise supporting evidence and examples to demonstrate that your statements are accurate. These examples need to be linked clearly to your argument.

You will have 40 minutes to write an answer to each question in the examination. In this time it is difficult to address every issue of some relevance to the question. Therefore, examiners will award full marks for answers that deal adequately, and in detail, with most of the central issues.

Russia in Revolution, 1881–1924: from Autocracy to Dictatorship is Topic D3 of Paper 6HI01/D, A World Divided: Communism and Democracy in the Twentieth Century. In the exam you will be required to answer questions relating to two different topics from Option D. This book deals exclusively with Topic D3.

The examination paper

The exam paper has seven topics, and you are required to answer questions on two of these topics. Each topic contains two questions and you can only choose one of these questions. The format of the topic questions in a typical examination paper is as follows:

> **6HI01/D — A World Divided: Communism and Democracy in the Twentieth Century**
>
> **Answer TWO questions: ONE question on each of the TWO topics for which you have been prepared. You may only answer ONE question on each topic.**
>
> **D3 — Russia in Revolution, 1881–1924: from Autocracy to Dictatorship**
>
> **EITHER**
>
> **9.** How stable was the tsarist regime by the outbreak of the First World War? **(Total: 30 marks)**
>
> **OR**
>
> **10.** To what extent was Russia's decision to continue to fight in the First World War the main reason for Lenin's victory in the Bolshevik Revolution? **(Total: 30 marks)**

Examinable skills

A total of 60 marks are available for Unit 1. Marks will be awarded for demonstrating the following skills:

- focusing on the requirements of the question, such as the topic, the period specified and the 'key concept'
- remembering, choosing and using historical knowledge
- analysing, explaining and reaching a judgement
- showing links between the key factors of your explanation

Focusing on the requirements of the question

Read the question carefully to ensure that you have noted the topic, the period and the key concept that is being addressed. One of the following concepts will be addressed by each question: causation, consequence, continuity, chance and significance.

In the following question:

How successful was Lenin in introducing communism in Russia by his death in 1924?

The topic is *the rule of Lenin*, the period is *1917–24* and the key concept is consequence — *explaining the success of Lenin's rule*.

Remembering, choosing and using historical knowledge

When you have established what the question requires, you must decide which aspects of your own knowledge are relevant. Examiners are looking for an answer that covers between four and six factors. Next, you must arrange these factors in a logical order to create a plan for your answer.

Once your structure is in place, you must develop it using specific examples. Try to ensure that your examples are detailed. You should include relevant dates; names of people, places, institutions and events; statistics and appropriate technical vocabulary. Examiners will reward both range and depth of knowledge.

Analysing, explaining and reaching a judgement

Telling the story of an event will not score well. It is expected that your answer will be arranged thematically, addressing different factors in turn.

Your key factors and supporting examples must be explicitly linked back to the question: that is to say, you must show how these details relate to or illustrate the argument that you are making. It is good practice to make these links at the end of each paragraph. It is also important that your essay reaches a clear judgement.

Showing links between the key factors of your explanation

In order to achieve the highest marks, you must highlight links between the factors that you have selected. This could mean demonstrating the relative importance of the different factors, or showing how the factors were dependent on each other.

Level descriptors

Answers are normally marked according to the five levels listed in the table below.

Level	Mark	Descriptor
1	1–6	Candidates produce mostly simple statements. These are supported by limited factual material that has some accuracy and relevance, although not directed at the focus of the question. The material is mostly generalised. There are few, if any, links between the simple statements. The writing may have limited coherence and is generally comprehensible, but passages lack both clarity and organisation. The skills needed to produce effective writing are not normally present. Frequent syntactical and/or spelling errors are likely to be present.
2	7–12	Candidates produce a series of simple statements supported by some mostly accurate and relevant factual material. The analytical focus is mostly implicit and there are likely to be only limited links between the simple statements. Material is unlikely to be developed very far. The writing has some coherence and is generally comprehensible, but passages lack both clarity and organisation. Some of the skills needed to produce effective writing are present. Frequent syntactical and/or spelling errors are likely to be present.
3	13–18	Candidates' answers attempt analysis and show some understanding of the focus of the question. However, they include material that either is descriptive, and thus only implicitly relevant to the question's focus, or which strays from that focus. Factual material will be accurate but it may lack depth and/or relevance in places. The writing is coherent in places but there are likely to be passages that lack clarity and/or proper organisation. Only some of the skills needed to produce convincing extended writing are likely to be present. Syntactical and/or spelling errors are likely to be present.
4	19–24	Candidates offer an analytical response that relates well to the focus of the question and shows some understanding of the key issues contained in it. The analysis is supported by accurate factual material that is mostly relevant to the question asked. The selection of material may lack balance in places. The answer shows some degree of direction and control but these attributes may not be sustained throughout the answer. The candidate demonstrates the skills needed to produce convincing extended writing but there may be passages that lack clarity or coherence. The answer is likely to include some syntactical and/or spelling errors.
5	25–30	Candidates offer an analytical response that directly addresses the focus of the question and demonstrates explicit understanding of the key issues contained in it. It is broadly balanced in its treatment of these key issues. The analysis is supported by accurate, relevant and appropriately selected factual material that demonstrates some range and depth. The exposition is controlled and the deployment logical. Some syntactical and/or spelling errors may be found but the writing is coherent overall. The skills required to produce convincing extended writing are in place.

How to use this guide

First, make sure that you understand the layout of the examination paper, the pattern of the marks and the types of question asked, all of which are explained above. Study the outline of the content required, which is given in the Content Guidance section. Try to:

- master the vocabulary and concepts given there
- establish clearly the important individuals and institutions which shaped the events of these years
- assess the extent of change between 1881 and 1924

The most important part of this guide is the Question and Answer section, which provides five examples of the kinds of question that you will be asked. It is important to work through these, studying the two sets of sample answers provided and the examiner's comments. The first answer to each question is an A-grade response which, although not perfect, gives a good idea of what is required. The purpose of the second answer is to illustrate some of the common errors made by students.

Content Guidance

Unit 1 of the Edexcel AS course focuses on historical themes. As these themes are covered in some breadth, it is important that you understand the topic over a period of time.

Option D3 examines Russia from 1881 to 1924. You have to be able to explain how Russia changed from an absolute monarchy under the tsar in the early period, through war and revolution, to the world's first Communist state. You need to know the political system under the later tsars and the major political, social, economic and foreign policy problems they faced.

You must understand how war in 1904–05 and 1914–17 impacted on the Russian state. You also need to understand why revolution took place in Russia in 1905, February 1917 and October 1917.

Finally, you are expected to be able explain how Lenin established a Communist government, the threats he faced and how he dealt with them.

Outline of topics

Russia in 1881: a survey

Russia's position in the world
The Russian political system
Social and economic problems

1881-1905: the making of the revolution

Alexander III's rule, 1881–94
Russian foreign policy, 1881–1905
Social and economic change, 1881–1905

The 1905 Revolution

Collective causes
Outcomes

1905-17: the downfall of the tsarist regime

Reform and repression in Russia, 1906–14
The impact of the First World War
The February Revolution, 1917

1917: the failure of the Provisional Government

Political and economic problems
The impact of Lenin's return to Russia
Lenin's ideas
The July days
The Kornilov Affair
The Bolshevik Revolution of October 1917

1917-24: Lenin in power

Problems facing Lenin in October 1917
The Treaty of Brest-Litovsk, 1918
Consolidation of power
Civil War, 1918–21
Introducing communism, 1918–21
Creating a Communist dictatorship by 1924

A note on the Russian calendar 1881–1918

Until 1918, Russia used the Julian calendar while the rest of Europe used the Gregorian calendar. The main difference was the fact that the Russian calendar was approximately 10 days behind the Gregorian calendar. Therefore, if you were in Britain, the February Revolution in Russia actually took place in March and the October Revolution took place in November. When Lenin took power, he changed the calendar to conform to the rest of Europe.

Russia in 1881: a survey

Russia's position in the world

In 1881, the Russian empire covered approximately 20% of the world's land surface. It stretched from modern day Poland in the west to the Pacific Ocean. It was over 80 times larger than the UK and twice the size of the world's next largest country, Canada. It was approximately 4,000 miles from the Baltic Sea in the west to the Pacific Ocean in the east and nearly 2,000 miles from Russia's Arctic territories to its borders with Iran in the south. This vast empire was dominated by the Russians; however, it contained a multitude of other races. In the west the empire encompassed Poles, Finns and Ukrainians. In the south it included Azeris, Armenians and Georgians. In the east it comprised Asiatic peoples such as Turkmens, Uzbeks, Kazakhs and Tartars. By 1881, the Russian speaking population comprised less than 50% of the population. The only census taken in imperial Russia occurred in 1897 — the total population was 125 million and Russian speakers comprised 55.5 million.

This vast empire had been created over the previous 200 years. Two great rulers stood out as major influences on the development of Russia. From 1682 to 1725, Peter the Great expanded the Russian state to the Black Sea in the south and the Baltic Sea in the west. He moved the capital from Moscow to **St Petersburg** and modernised Russia, adopting western European customs and methods of administration. The other key ruler was Catherine the Great (1762–96), who established Russia as a major European power. From 1812 to 1814, Russia was important in bringing about the defeat of Napoleon and by 1815, Russia possessed Europe's largest army.

In 1881, Russia was one of the five European **great powers**, along with Britain, France, Germany and Austria-Hungary. It was also a major colonial empire, covering much of the eastern and northern parts of the Eurasian landmass. Yet Russia still had major foreign policy ambitions.

From the 1850s to 1881, Russia expanded its control over central Asia. By 1881, it had reached the borders of Afghanistan, coming into conflict with Britain, which controlled modern day India and Pakistan. In the east, Russia had ambitions to extend its control into northern China. In southeast Europe, Russia wished to extend its political influence in the Balkan Peninsula and to gain permission to send warships from the Black Sea to the Mediterranean Sea through the Straits of the Bosporus and the Dardanelles, which were controlled by the Ottoman empire.

As a great power, Russia played a large role in European affairs before 1881 and attended all major European conferences from 1814. It was in close alliance with Germany and Austria-Hungary and in 1873, Russia joined with these two in the *Dreikaiserbund* or Three Emperors' League. The three great powers made a joint declaration to uphold the rule of monarchy.

In the mid-1870s, Russia came into conflict with Austria-Hungary over rival claims to Balkan territory and the *Dreikaiserbund* of 1873 came to an end. However, in 1881, a new Three Emperors' Alliance was formed which attempted to resurrect the earlier agreement. This new agreement only lasted until 1887, when renewed international tension in the Balkans again brought Russia into conflict with Austria-Hungary. Germany attempted to stay in alliance with Russia with the Reinsurance Treaty of 1887–90. However, Germany refused to renew the treaty in 1890 and after that date Russia sought a new ally — Germany's enemy, France.

The Russian political system

Russia was the most conservative and reactionary of all the major European states. At the top of the Russian political system stood the tsar of all the Russias; as emperor he had absolute political power. At his coronation, the tsar was seen as appointed by God to rule, and each successive tsar believed he was answerable only to God for his political actions. Under this form of government the tsar chose and dismissed all his ministers; each minister was individually responsible to the tsar. The tsar ruled through Imperial Decree or *ukaz*. There was no national parliament or national elections and no legal political parties. With such enormous political power embodied in one person, the personality and skill of the tsar were central to the success or failure of the Russian government.

From 1855 to 1881 Russia was ruled by Alexander II and, like his predecessor Peter the Great, he wished to modernise Russia. From 1855 to his assassination by political extremists in 1881, he made major reforms to local government, the judicial system and the armed forces. However, his most significant reform was the emancipation of the serfs in 1861.

As well as choosing all government ministers, the tsar was commander-in-chief of the armed forces and had control over foreign policy. He also appointed provincial governors, each responsible for administering a part of the vast empire. In 1864, Tsar Alexander II established *zemstva* (*zemstvo* in the singular), which were elected local government committees responsible for issues such as road maintenance and local elementary education. The right to vote for *zemstva* was strictly limited to the educated classes. In 1870, this form of elected local government was extended to towns. In 1881, Alexander II planned to set up a national elected parliament but he was assassinated on his way to sign the decree.

Two important institutions helped maintain the tsarist system of government. One was the armed forces; they maintained law and order and repressed any political dissent. The other institution was the Russian Orthodox Church, the official religion of the Russian empire. The tsar was not only seen as head of state and government but also head of the church. Most Russians were followers of the Russian Orthodox Church. However, non-Russians followed a variety of religions such as Roman Catholicism among the Poles and Lithuanians and Islam among the peoples of central Asia. In the area now known as Belarus there was a large Jewish population.

The tsarist political system was under threat from a variety of groups. Many of the educated middle class hoped that Russia would follow a political path similar to other great powers in central and western Europe. They wished to see an elected national parliament and freedom of the press. They wanted the tsar to become a constitutional monarch similar to Britain's Queen Victoria. Other groups had more extreme aims. Some wished to remove the tsar altogether as a prelude to major social and economic change, where political and economic power would be passed to former serfs.

In a multi-racial empire like Russia there were nationalist groups who wanted their own independent state. The most significant ethnic group which sought separation were the Poles, who had revolted against Russian rule in 1830 and 1863 in bids to create an independent Poland. Finally, perhaps the most extreme political group were the Nihilists, who simply wanted to rid Russia of the tsar as a prelude to a new political system which they believed was bound to be an improvement. It was a group of Nihilists that assassinated Alexander II in 1881.

Social and economic problems

Compared to other major European states in 1881, the Russian empire was regarded as backward in social and economic development. Before 1861, approximately 80% of the Russian population were agricultural labourers who did not own land. They either worked for the state (tsar) or private landowners. Since the fifteenth century, these labourers owed obligations to their landowners. They had to work for nothing on landowners' estates and had major restrictions on where they could live and whom they could marry.

As a result, these labourers were not free but were serfs. Serfdom was seen as a major restriction on the modernisation of Russia. Similar social systems had occurred in western and central Europe since the **Middle Ages**. However, the last aspects of serfdom in central Europe had disappeared after the 1848 revolutions. In the Emancipation Decree of March 1861, Alexander II brought serfdom to an end. In compensation to their former landowners, all serfs were expected to make redemption payments that would pay for their freedom. After 1861, most serfs continued to live in villages and were subject to the authority of village elders who acted as a ruling committee. The village elders had the power to redistribute land between former serfs; to leave a village, a former serf had to get the elders' permission.

Economically, the Russian empire was predominantly agricultural. In 1897, it had only two cities with over 1 million inhabitants: the capital St Petersburg and Moscow. In southern Russia and Ukraine, vast grasslands, known as the steppes, produced grain, much of which was exported. However, many former serfs engaged in subsistence agriculture which limited the amount of agricultural goods produced by the Russian economy. In times of poor harvest subsistence farmers were also vulnerable to food shortages and famine; in 1891 a major famine occurred in southern Russia.

Russia did possess industry but this tended to be located in cities in western Russia, such as St Petersburg and Moscow. In eastern Ukraine, coal was mined in the Donbass region. Yet the economic and industrial potential of Russia was enormous. In many ways Russia in 1881 resembled the USA in the same year. The USA had its 'wild West', with vast reserves of timber and of metals such as copper, gold and silver. Russia had Siberia, a vast, sparsely populated area of northern Asia but, unlike the USA, Russia lacked the transport infrastructure to exploit its potential wealth; Russia only had railways in the west of the empire. Much of the empire was joined together by dirt roads, which froze in the winter and became mud in spring. The main artery of trade and communication was the river system. However, the majority of Siberia's rivers flowed south to north into the Arctic Ocean.

In social and economic terms Russia was a sleeping giant. If Russia were able to tap into the potential of its population and natural resources, it would become one of the world's greatest powers.

Glossary

great power: between 1815 and 1914 there were five great powers in Europe: Britain, France, Russia and Austria-Hungary. Great power status was determined by military power. By the late nineteenth century, military power was linked increasingly to economic power. Russian governmental involvement in encouraging economic growth was linked directly to the need to maintain Russia's great power status.

Middle Ages: a period of European history from the fall of the Roman empire in the fifth century to the end of the fifteenth century.

St Petersburg: the capital of Russia from the early eighteenth century. When the First World War broke out, the name was changed to its Russian version, Petrograd. Following Lenin's death in January 1924, the city was renamed Leningrad in his honour. It was renamed St Petersburg in the 1990s.

1881–1905: the making of the revolution

Alexander III's rule, 1881–94

Alexander II ruled Russia from 1855 to his death in 1881 and was called the 'tsar liberator' because of his reforms — in particular, the emancipation of the serfs. However, Tsar **Alexander III** was known for his repressive policies and no doubt a major contributory factor in these policies was the circumstances of his accession to power. His father, Alexander II, had been assassinated by political extremists and so Alexander III began his reign with a clampdown on all political opposition to tsarism.

By nature, Alexander III was an autocrat who believed fervently that he had a God-given right to rule Russia. He was also a devout follower of the Russian Orthodox Church and viewed with great suspicion the followers of other religions. He relied for advice on a leading figure in the Russian Orthodox Church, **Konstantin Pobedonostsev**. Pobedonostev was the chief procurator of the Holy Synod of the Russian Orthodox Church and was Alexander III's minister for church affairs. Like Alexander III, he believed in tsarism and the dominant role of the Orthodox Church in Russian society; between them they attempted to squash any political dissent.

Restoring political control

The first victim of Alexander III's rule were the Loris-Melikov reforms, named after the person Tsar Alexander II had appointed to bring further political reform — Count Loris-Melikov. These reforms included a plan to establish a national consultative assembly to advise the tsar on legislation and would have formed the basis of Russia's first constitution. However, Alexander III did not carry out the reforms and dismissed Loris-Melikov. On 14 August 1881, the tsar issued the statute on Measures to Preserve National Order and Public Peace. This was originally intended to be a temporary law passed in the wake of Alexander II's assassination but it was renewed every 3 years until the February Revolution of 1917. Initially, Alexander III dismissed those officials across the empire suspected of 'liberal' ideas. However, this new law gave the police enormous power to arrest, imprison and exile political opponents of the tsar. The force given responsibility for enforcing the law was the **Okhrana**, the Russian secret police. In 1887, a law on universities was implemented after the discovery of a plot among university students to assassinate Alexander III. It established strict government control over their operation. The main targets of the *Okhrana* were extremist political groups. The Nihilist Group, founded in 1879 and also called People's Will, was responsible for Alexander II's death. The *Okhrana* arrested the main culprits involved in Alexander II's assassination and these were subsequently executed. Other followers of extremist groups fled Russia before they could be arrested, with many settling in London.

In 1889, an important aspect of the new repression was the appointment of land captains. These were centrally appointed officials who replaced the local justices of the peace in the administration of law. In 1890, land captains became members of the *zemstva*; they also ensured that Alexander III's new repressive laws were enforced. For instance, land captains could close down newspapers deemed critical of the government. Further change in 1890 meant that the *zemstva* also had their powers limited. By the time of his death in 1894, Alexander III had won back much of the political control that his reformist predecessor had granted to other bodies. Alexander III had recreated absolute rule by the tsar.

In an attempt to bring greater conformity and cohesion to his empire, Alexander III adopted a policy of Russification. The idea was to ensure that the Russian language, spoken by less than 50% of the population, would become the official language of the state. A form of Russification was introduced by Alexander II following the Polish Revolt of 1863, but Alexander III made it a major policy covering the whole empire. In many ways it could be seen as a logical step to ensure a degree of cohesion in such a vast multi-ethnic empire. However, the implementation of Russification was resented by many ethnic groups, which saw it as a policy that repressed national identity.

An aspect of Alexander III's nationalist policies, which had a strong element of racial prejudice, was his actions against the empire's Jewish population. According to the 1897 census, Jews comprised just 5.2% of the empire's population. However, much of the Jewish population was concentrated in western Russia in an area known as the Jewish Pale (which is in modern-day Belarus). Both Alexander III and Konstantin Pobedonostev were anti-Semites. In the early 1890s, the Russian authorities organised mob violence — known as pogroms — against Jewish villages. Jews were accused of engaging in a worldwide conspiracy against Russia. Tens of thousands of Russian Jews fled in the wake of the pogroms, many emigrating to the USA and Britain.

To ensure the preservation of the Christian basis of the Russian state, Pobedonostsev put all *zemstva*-controlled primary schools under the control of the Russian Orthodox Church. All children, irrespective of their religious background, were forced to learn about the Russian Orthodox religion.

By the time of his death in 1894, Alexander III had turned the political clock back in Russia. Instead of moving towards a western European style constitutional monarchy, in 1894 Russia resembled the absolute monarchies of mid-eighteenth century Europe. Across Europe thousands of political exiles worked to overthrow a Russian political system they despised. Within Russia, in Siberia, thousands of other political prisoners were forced to accept internal exile far away from the towns and cities of western Russia.

However, the reign of Alexander III was not completely bleak and repressive; some reforms took place in the economy. In 1887, **Ivan Vyshnegradsky** became minister of finance. He allowed peasants financial incentives to move to new virgin lands in Siberia as a way to populate and develop that vast region; he also acquired foreign loans to help develop Russia economically. It was during his period as finance minister that plans were drawn up to build a Trans-Siberian Railway, which would provide the transport infrastructure necessary to exploit Siberia's great economic potential. Yet these reforms failed to prevent a major famine that hit southern Russia in 1891, when tens of thousands died of starvation. The famine increased resentment against tsarist rule, so that when Nicholas II became tsar in 1894, he faced major social, economic and political problems, far greater than any other ruler of a major European state at that time.

Russian foreign policy, 1881–1905

In 1881, Russia was both a major European power and a major global colonial power and had a number of areas of interest across Eurasia. In Europe, Russia was a great power, in alliance with Germany and Austria-Hungary in the *Dreikaiserbund* or Three Emperors' League. In southeast Europe, Russia harboured expansionist plans to increase its influence at the expense of Ottoman Turkey. In central Asia, Russia had conquered a number of Islamic states in the period 1855–81 and had ambitions to acquire territory at the expense of Afghanistan. This brought Russia into direct conflict with Britain, which possessed a large colonial empire in modern-day India and Pakistan. Finally, Russia was increasingly interested in expanding its influence in the far east at the expense of the weak Chinese empire. This would also bring Russia into conflict with Britain, but, more importantly, with the rising power of Japan.

Russia's main area of interest in Europe was the **Balkan Peninsula** in the southeast. For the period prior to 1881, much of the Balkan Peninsula was under the political control of the Ottoman empire. However, in 1881, the Ottoman empire was militarily and economically weak and found it increasingly difficult to keep control over its Balkan possessions. What made matters worse for the Ottoman empire was the fact that the population of the Balkans was largely Christian and comprised a variety of ethnic groups who wished to be free from Balkan control. In addition, on the northern borders of the Balkans were two great powers that wished to expand their influence on the peninsula. In the northwest was Austria-Hungary. To the northeast was Russia, which hoped to gain influence over the Balkan Peninsula and gain control of the Straits of the Bosporus and Dardanelles so Russian warships could travel between the Black Sea and the Mediterranean Sea.

Between 1875 and 1878, a major international crisis arose over the Balkans. Uprisings by ethnic minorities in the Balkans against Ottoman rule escalated into a war between the Ottoman empire and two small Balkan states, Serbia and Montenegro. In 1877, Russia entered the war on the side of Serbia and Montenegro. In 1878, having won the war, Russia attempted to impose a peace settlement which greatly favoured Russia. Both Britain and Austria-Hungary vehemently opposed the peace and forced Russia to accept a less favourable peace in the Treaty of Berlin of 1878. The Balkan Crisis of 1875–78 fractured the Three Emperors' Agreement. In 1881, the German chancellor, Bismarck, attempted to patch up differences between Russia and Austria-Hungary by drawing up the Three Emperors' Alliance. However, another Balkan crisis arose in 1885 over Bulgaria, which saw Austria-Hungary and Russia supporting opposing sides. The Three Emperors' Alliance came to an end in 1887. Bismarck attempted a secret Russo–German alliance — the Reinsurance Treaty — that lasted until 1890.

After 1890, when Germany refused to renew the treaty, Russia sought a new ally. In 1893, Russia signed a secret alliance with France, Germany's enemy. From 1893 to the First World War in 1914, Europe was divided into two armed camps. On one side was the Triple Alliance of Germany, Austria-Hungary and Italy; on the other was the Dual Alliance of France and Russia. Partly as a result of this stalemate in Europe, Russia sought to expand its influence in Asia.

In the 1880s, Russia acquired territory at the expense of Afghanistan in the areas of Merv and Penjdeh. However, these developments were opposed by Britain, which feared that Russia wished to control all Afghanistan and then have a common border with the British Indian empire. During the period 1886 to the First World War, a stalemate occurred in central Asia, with both Britain and Russia attempting to gain influence over Afghanistan.

The far east
The main area of Russian expansion in the 1890s was in the far east. This coincided with two developments.

- First, the construction of the Trans-Siberian Railway allowed Russia, for the first time, to have an effective overland transport link with its far eastern territories.
- Second, the Chinese empire was widely regarded by contemporaries as being on the verge of collapse and disintegration. Russia, like other powers such as Britain, France, Germany and Japan, wished to acquire Chinese territory. These developments led directly to a confrontation between Russia and Japan in northern China, which erupted into war in 1904.

A major issue facing Russia in the far east was the acquisition of a seaport which was ice-free all year round. Russia's main seaport in the far east was Vladivostok, which was not open to shipping at the height of winter. Russia was also interested in the raw materials available in northern China, in particular in Korea and in the province of Manchuria, which possessed coal and oil. Finally, the province of Manchuria stood between Siberia and the southern part of Russia's far-eastern province. Russia wanted to acquire rights from China to build a railway across Manchuria, linking Vladivostok with Siberia. By 1904, Russia had been successful in meeting many of these aims. It had acquired control over the Chinese seaport of Port Arthur in southern Manchuria, giving it an ice-free port, and had acquired permission to build the North Chinese Railway linking Siberia and Vladivostok.

Russo–Japanese War

However, Russia faced a rival in its desire to win economic influence over Manchuria and Korea in the form of Japan. The Japanese empire had gone through a rapid period of modernisation since the 1860s. In this period Japan began to industrialise and modernise its armed forces. From 1894 to 1895, Japan defeated China to acquire Taiwan and gain influence in Korea. In 1904, both Russia and Japan hoped to gain influence over Manchuria and Korea. This mutual aim led directly to war between the two powers.

In February 1904, the war began with a Japanese surprise attack on the Russian seaport and naval base of Port Arthur that destroyed the Russian Pacific Fleet. Japanese army units then invaded Manchuria and came into conflict with Russian forces defending the North Chinese Railway and Russian economic interests. At the Battle of Mukden, the Japanese defeated Russian forces and began to occupy Manchuria.

The war led to a wave of national enthusiasm in Russia. It was widely believed that the Japanese would be no match for the Russian armed forces. Reinforcements were sent via the Trans-Siberian Railway to confront the Japanese in Manchuria. A more ambitious plan was to dispatch the Russian Baltic Fleet to the far east. It took that fleet from October 1904 to May 1905 to make the 18,000-mile voyage. On route at Dogger Bank in the North Sea, the Russians mistook the Hull and Grimsby fishing fleets for Japanese torpedo boats and opened fire, causing several deaths and the loss of a number of trawlers. After arriving in the Straits of Tsushima, which separate Japan from Korea, the Russian Baltic Fleet, under Admiral Zinovy Rozhestvensky, was heavily defeated by the Japanese under Admiral Togo. Five Russian battleships, two cruisers and five destroyers were sunk and 4,300 Russian sailors were killed. The Japanese lost three torpedo boats and 177 men killed.

The war and, in particular, the Battle of Tsushima, were seen as a national humiliation. Russia had been defeated by an 'oriental race' and had lost most of its navy. The war came to an end with the Treaty of Portsmouth (USA) on 5 September 1905. Under the treaty, Russia evacuated all its troops from Manchuria. Japan took over Port Arthur and the surrounding Chinese territory of the Liaodong Peninsula. Japan also received from Russia the southern end of the island of Sakhalin, north of Japan. The war also meant that Japan would be the dominant foreign power in Korea, which joined the Japanese empire in 1910.

The Russo–Japanese War undermined the tsarist regime; it was a major defeat. The war fuelled resentment against the tsar and helped to create the political conditions for the outbreak of revolution in Russia in 1905. However, to most Russians the war was a colonial affair, far away from Russia's heartland. Although the Russian armed forces were defeated in the far east, they remained loyal to the tsarist regime.

Social and economic change, 1881–1905

In the years 1881–1905, Russian society went through a major social and economic transformation. In 1881, Russia was a predominantly agricultural country with 80% of its population living as peasants, many engaged in subsistence agriculture. Although a vast country with a large population, Russia was the most economically backward of the five European great powers. However, by 1905, Russia had begun to industrialise and to exploit the great economic potential of Siberia.

Sergei Witte

A key factor in the economic change facing Russia was the appointment of **Sergei Witte** to the tsar's government. He became minister of ways and communications in 1892 and minister of finance in 1893 — a post he held until 1903. In that decade, Witte laid the foundations for the economic transformation of Russia. During this time Russia also began to industrialise rapidly in centres such as St Petersburg, Moscow, Ukraine and Baku. The centrepiece of Witte's period as minister of finance was the construction of the Trans-Siberian Railway. This railway was constructed to link the capital, St Petersburg, on the Baltic Sea with Vladivostok on the Pacific Ocean, a distance of 4,500 miles. It was the Russian equivalent of the construction of the transcontinental railways across the USA. It was hoped that the Trans-Siberian Railway would have a similar effect in opening up the vast potential of Siberia for both settlement and mineral extraction.

A major obstacle to Russian economic development before the 1890s was the lack of funds to finance industrial growth. Witte adopted a range of methods to raise funds. Like his predecessor, Vyschnegradsky, he raised foreign loans mainly from France, Germany and Britain. France provided the greatest amount, comprising 33% of all the foreign loans. Investors were attracted by the possibility of earning financial rewards from the exploitation of Siberia's resources. Witte also ensured that the Russian state played a key role in encouraging economic development. This was a key feature of economic development, both in the last years of tsarist Russia and under Communist rule from 1917. Finally, Witte increased taxation on the peasantry. This caused considerable resentment, in particular at times of poor harvests, and was a contributory factor to spontaneous peasant uprisings in the early years of the twentieth century.

The impact of Witte's reforms was impressive: coal production rose from 6,000 tons per year in 1890 to 16,000 by 1900. Oil production rose from 3,800 tons to 10,600 tons in the same period; iron and steel production leapt from 2,000 tons in 1890 to 8,200 tons in 1900. In St Petersburg large factories developed, such as the Putilov Engineering Works. On the Caspian Sea, in the south near the Iranian border, an oil industry developed around the city of Baku. However, even though Russia went through a process of rapid industrialisation, by the outbreak of the First World War, the gross domestic product was still below that of the other great powers.

The rapid industrialisation of Russia brought with it a movement of the population from the countryside to industrial areas. By the early twentieth century, Russia had a sizeable industrial working class. The industrial workforce rose from 1.4 million workers in 1890 to 2.6 million in 1906. This was still a small proportion of the Russian population, which numbered 125 million in 1897. These workers lived and worked in poor conditions and resentment towards their plight led to demonstrations and strikes.

In the countryside the Russian population rose rapidly in the last half of the nineteenth century and this put pressure on landholdings. To meet the rise in population, village communes redistributed land. As a result, average peasant landholdings in European Russia fell from 35 acres (14.5 hectares) in 1877 to only 28 acres (11 hectares) in 1905. This development took place at a time of rising taxes on the peasantry and periodic outbreaks of famine. Famines occurred in European Russia in 1891, 1892, 1898 and 1901.

This resulted in the peasantry's growing resentment towards oppressive government taxation and lower yields from their landholdings. A result was the outbreak of *jacqueries*. These were spontaneous peasant uprisings, when peasants attacked landowners and their property, usually to destroy records of rent arrears. Many *jacqueries* were extremely violent.

Therefore, Witte's period as finance minister brought considerable economic advancement but it also resulted in the rise of social problems, both in the towns and countryside. Resentment of the tsarist system of government had developed by the early years of the twentieth century. Workers resented poor living and working conditions, high taxation and smaller landholdings. A wide variety of the middle class resented the autocratic system of government under the tsar. Russia seemed primed for revolution.

Glossary

Balkan Peninsula: a peninsula in southeast Europe which comprises the present-day states of Romania, Bulgaria, Albania, Serbia, Montenegro, Macedonia, Greece, Croatia and European Turkey.

***Okhrana*:** created in 1880 to replace the Third Department. It was officially known as the Department for the Defence of Public Security and Order. Its main task was to deal with political opponents of the tsar. It was dissolved by the Provisional Government following the February Revolution of 1917.

Key figures

Alexander II (1818–81): came to the throne at the age of 36 in the middle of the Crimean War against Britain and France. Following Russia's defeat in the Crimean War, he embarked on a series of radical reforms as a way of modernising Russia. The most significant was the Emancipation of the Serfs in 1861, for which he was regarded as the 'tsar liberator'.

Alexander III (1845–94): succeeded his father, Alexander II, in 1881. He was tutored and advised by Konstantin Pobedonostev, which made him an arch-conservative. Following his father's assassination, he engaged in reactionary policies to stamp out opposition to tsardom.

Konstantin Pobedonostsev (1827–1907): the leading supporter of Russian conservatism in the last quarter of the nineteenth century. He had a major influence over Alexander III and his son Nicholas II. A professor of civil law, in 1880, during his early career, he became chief procurator of the Holy Synod of the Russian Orthodox Church. The Holy Synod was the senior assembly of the Russian Orthodox clergy. In this position he was the government's leading spokesman on religious affairs.

Ivan Vyshnegradsky (1831–97): finance minister 1887–92. By the time he became a government minister, he had already amassed a vast fortune in his career as an engineer and businessman. He supported greater government involvement in the economy, in particular in railway development. He left office in 1892 for health reasons.

Sergei Witte (1849–1915): born in Georgia in southern Russia, a descendent of Dutch immigrants. Initially involved in railway administration, he joined the government in 1892 and became minister of finance in 1893. He was held responsible for the 'Great Spurt' — the rapid industrialisation of Russia in the 1890s and early twentieth century. He was transferred to chair the committee of ministers until 1905. During that period the tsar asked him to be part of the negotiating team appointed to end the Russo–Japanese War. He returned again to high office as Russian prime minister following the outbreak of the 1905 Revolution. He advocated the October Manifesto, which the tsar adopted.

The 1905 Revolution

Collective causes

Bloody Sunday

On 22 January 1905, approximately 150,000 workers from factories across St Petersburg assembled outside the Winter Palace. They demonstrated peacefully and wanted to present the tsar with a petition of their grievances in the hope that he would do something about their poor living and working conditions. Unfortunately the tsar was not at home, he was staying at another residence outside St Petersburg at Tsarskoye Selo. Instead, the demonstrators were met by a cordon of troops that fired on the crowd — perhaps accidentally — but the result was panic and approximately 1,000 people died. A Russian Orthodox priest called **Father Gapon** led the demonstrators. He had helped to organise the Assembly of Russian Factory Workers in 1903, which became one of the largest worker organisations in St Petersburg. It has been alleged that Father Gapon was also a paid agent of the *Okhrana*, the secret police. The suspicion of this double role led to his assassination by political extremists in 1906.

The political impact of what became known as Bloody Sunday was immense. It sparked off strikes and demonstrations across Russia. By the early spring, Russia was engulfed in revolution that involved riots, peasant uprisings, mutinies in the armed forces and a rise in political activism. The tsar's hold on Russia seemed to be hanging by a thread. However, although Bloody Sunday was the immediate cause of the 1905 Revolution, there were much deeper, more significant causes.

Social and political discontent

First, Russia faced a major social and economic crisis by 1905. The rural population had risen rapidly, peasant landholdings had shrunk and government taxation had risen. With famines occurring in the 1890s and 1901, the Russian countryside was riven with dissent. The events of Bloody Sunday helped spark off widespread peasant protests across European Russia.

Second, the rapid industrialisation of Russia had created a sizeable industrial working class, centred mainly in towns, where they lived and worked in poor conditions. The growth of working organisations and strikes in the period prior to 1905 suggested that some form of social protest in industrial cities was inevitable.

Third, Russian reverses in the Russo–Japanese War of 1904–05 undermined support for the government. Russian army and naval forces were humiliated by the Japanese attacks on Korea and Manchuria. This was the most serious military defeat suffered by the Russian armed forces since the Crimean War of 1854–56.

Fourth, perhaps the most significant cause of the 1905 Revolution was the growing dissatisfaction with the tsarist system of government. Although political parties were officially banned in Russia before the 1905 Revolution, this ban did not stop the development of a wide variety of political opponents of tsarism coming together to form political organisations and groups.

Liberals

The Liberals were a moderate political grouping who came from the professional middle class. The Liberals wanted Russia to follow a political path similar to that of Western Europe. They wished to see an elected national parliament that would share power with the tsar in a constitutional monarchy. They also wished to see the activities of the *Okhrana* curtailed and to see greater freedom of the press. Many Liberals had become involved in the *zemstva* and an important national organisation for their opinions was the National Association of *Zemstva*.

Social Revolutionaries

The Social Revolutionary Party (the SRs) was founded in 1900 but its political and socio-economic ideas went back to the nineteenth century. The SRs saw the Russian peasantry as the true people of Russia, who should have control over Russia's land and play a central role in the government of the country. The SR Party's leader, Victor Chernov, hoped to widen the party's appeal through the inclusion of industrial workers. Given its ideas, the SRs were seen as a dangerous radical group full of political extremists who wished to destroy tsarism. The official view was correct, in the sense that the SRs had an extremist wing that wished to achieve its political ends through violence. These were the political heirs to People's Will, who had assassinated Tsar Alexander II in 1881. In the lead-up to the 1905 Revolution, SR terrorists assassinated Vyacheslav Plehve, the minister of the interior in 1904 and Grand Duke Sergei, the tsar's uncle, during the early months of 1905.

Social Democrats

Like the SRs, the Social Democrats wished to bring about a complete social and political transformation of Russia. Founded in Minsk (in modern-day Belarus), the Social Democrats looked for inspiration from the German left-wing thinker and writer **Karl Marx**. Social Democrats believed that the industrialisation of society would create two mutually hostile social classes: the bourgeoisie (factory owners and businessmen) and the proletariat (industrial working class). Eventually the proletariat would overthrow the bourgeoisie and create a just and equal society where economic wealth would be shared.

To Social Democrats, the European countries most likely to see a socialist revolution first were advanced industrial countries like Britain and Germany. However, following Witte's reform of the 1890s, a sizeable Russian working class was developing, which the Social Democrats believed would lead a Russian socialist revolution.

The extreme views of the Social Democrats meant they were prime targets for the *Okhrana*, so many Social Democrats lived abroad. In 1903, at their second congress which was held in London, the Social Democrats split into two major factions. One group — subsequently known as Mensheviks — believed membership of the party should be open to all who showed sympathy with their aims. Another faction — the Bolsheviks, led by **Vladimir Lenin** — believed party membership should be restricted to committed revolutionaries. Although Mensheviks and Bolsheviks shared the same ultimate aims, they began to operate as separate factions within the same party from 1903.

National groups

The Russian empire was a multi-racial empire and within its borders were ethnic groups who wished to gain either independence or self-government from Russia or to protect their own ethnic group from persecution. In the nineteenth century the most active national group were the Poles, who wished to re-establish an independent Polish state.

On two occasions, during 1830–32 and in 1863, nationalist revolts against Russian rule occurred in Poland and on each occasion they were brutally suppressed. Supported by Polish exiles in countries such as France, Polish nationalists within Russian Poland continued to work for Polish independence. Their support increased following the introduction of Alexander III's Russification programme in the 1890s.

Another group that wished to overthrow tsarist rule were Jews. They had been subjected to official persecution by the tsarist government in the 1890s. Many Jews joined radical organisations such as the Social Democrats, where they formed their own autonomous organisation called the Jewish Bund.

Outcomes

Strikes and uprisings

To virtually all political groups, the outbreak of strikes, demonstrations and peasant uprisings came as a surprise. However, shortly after the outbreak of unrest, leaders of the various political groups who disliked tsarism began to use the situation for their own advantage.

The 1905 Revolution was characterised by strikes and peasant uprisings. Strikes occurred throughout 1905, culminating in a general strike from 20 September to 2 October. The tsarist authorities struggled to keep law and order. Their task was made more difficult by mutinies in the armed forces. The most famous mutiny took place aboard the battleship *Potemkin* in the Black Sea Fleet. The crew took command of the ship in the naval base of Odessa and sailed it to neighbouring Romania.

However, much of the unrest associated with the revolution was spontaneous and lacked coordination; this allowed the tsarist authorities to retain control. They were aided by the bulk of the army in this task, which remained loyal to Tsar Nicholas II throughout the revolution. There were some important political developments. In October 1905, as part of the general strike, an assembly of workers called the St Petersburg Soviet was formed. It acted as a form of workers' parliament, articulating their grievances. The chairperson was the Social Democrat revolutionary **Leon Trotsky**, who had returned from exile in the USA to take part in the revolution. The soviet's existence was short-lived and it was disbanded by the tsarist authorities by early December. However, it did set a precedent for future workers' assemblies in 1917.

Failure of a revolution

Ultimately, the 1905 Revolution failed. It had lacked a clear leadership, and apart from a dislike of the tsarist regime, it also lacked a clear set of aims. Tsar Nicholas II followed the advice of his ministers and, in October 1905, issued a manifesto promising political reform. The October Manifesto promised the creation of a national elected parliament which would have a role in passing laws. It also proposed freedom of speech and freedom of religion. The manifesto split the political opposition. Many Liberals welcomed and supported these proposed reforms.

The promises of the October Manifesto were embodied in the Fundamental Law of 1906. This became the first real constitution for the Russian empire; it created a national parliament. The Upper House was called the Council of State, which was partly elected and partly nominated by the tsar. The Lower House was called the State Duma and was elected. However, the tsar retained the right to appoint and dismiss all ministers and under Article 87, he reserved the right to rule by decree, thereby ignoring parliament.

The Fundamental Law pleased conservative-minded Liberals, who, from 1906, were called Octobrists. Other Liberals hoped that the Fundamental Law would be the beginning of a gradual process towards a constitutional monarchy like Britain. These became known as Constitutional Democrats or Kadets.

Neither the October Manifesto nor the Fundamental Law pleased the SRs or Social Democrats. These political groups were targeted by the armed forces and *Okhrana* for arrest and imprisonment. They were aided by conservative supporters of the tsarist regime, who formed themselves into vigilante groups known as the Black Hundreds or the Union of Russian People. The Black Hundreds used the same terrorist style tactics as those of the extremist SRs and Social Democrats.

The 1905 Revolution failed to topple the tsar and his regime. However, it did bring some limited political reform and in some ways acted as a dress rehearsal for the February Revolution of 1917, which did succeed in overthrowing tsarism. It also led to a major backlash and clampdown on radical political activity, forcing the majority of SR and Social Democrat leaders to flee abroad for safety.

Key figures

Father Gapon (1870–1906): from a wealthy family, he decided to become a Russian Orthodox priest following the death of his wife in 1898. He preached and ministered in the poorer districts of St Petersburg. However, he came into conflict with Church authorities over incidents of gambling and drinking. He helped organise the Assembly of Russian Factory Workers, a body that was privately financed by the *Okhrana*. He led the demonstrators on Bloody Sunday but fled Russia after the event. He returned following the publication of the October Manifesto. He was accused of being an agent of the *Okhrana* and was hanged by political extremists in 1906.

Vladimir Lenin (1870–1924): born Vladimir Ulyanov into a wealthy family living in Simbirsk. He had German and Kalmyk ancestors. In 1887, his elder brother was executed for his part in an attempted assassination of Alexander III. He was a founder member of the Russian Social Democrat Party in 1898. He founded a revolutionary newspaper, *Iskra* (*The Spark*), while living in London. To cover his true identity, he also took the nickname of Lenin, meaning 'man from the Lean River'. He founded the Bolshevik Party, which later became the Communist Party. He advocated the overthrow of the Provisional Government from April 1917 and was the leading force behind the October Revolution of 1917. He was leader of Communist Russia from 1917 until his death in January 1924. However, from 1922 he was incapacitated, following a stroke.

Karl Marx (1818–83): born in Trier, in the Rhineland of Germany, a philosopher and political activist who founded Marxism, the basis of modern socialism and communism. He lived most of his later life in London. Marx believed human history was a series of conflicts between competing social and economic classes, which would lead ultimately to the creation of a classless Communist society.

Leon Trotsky (1879–1940): born Lev Bronstein, he became involved in revolutionary activity as a teenager and spent time in internal exile in Siberia. He escaped from Siberia in 1902 and joined the Social Democrats. Like Lenin, he took a nickname to hide his true identity. He went into exile in the USA but returned to Russia following the 1905 Revolution and became the chairperson of the St Petersburg Soviet. He originally stood apart from the split between the Mensheviks and Bolsheviks but decided to join the Bolsheviks in the summer of 1917. He led the All-Russia Soviet Military Revolutionary Committee, which organised the Bolshevik seizure of power.

From October 1917, Trotsky was a regular member of the Politburo, the leading decision-making body of the Communist Party. He was minister of war and founder of the Red Army. He was the major military leader of the Reds in the Civil War. Widely tipped to be Lenin's successor, he was out-manoeuvred by Stalin. Trotsky was dismissed from the Politburo in 1925 and forced into exile in 1928. He was assassinated by a Stalinist agent in Mexico City in 1940.

1905–17: the downfall of the tsarist regime

Reform and repression in Russia, 1906–14

The tsarist regime survived the trauma of the 1905 Revolution. In the period between 1906 and the outbreak of the First World War in 1914, Russia went through a period of political repression and social and economic reform.

State duma

The promise of political reform bore fruit with the election to the first state duma in April 1906. The right to vote was limited to literate men; nevertheless, the elections produced a large number of deputies who wanted further political reform, including the release of political prisoners. Faced with these demands, the tsar dissolved the state duma after just 73 days. A second set of elections took place for another state duma, which met in February 1907. Unfortunately for the tsar, the composition of the state duma reflected a demand for further substantial reform. It lasted until June 1907, when the tsar dissolved it, claiming it was a hotbed of subversion.

In November 1907, a new state duma was elected on a restricted franchise limited to the wealthy. It contained a majority of deputies who supported the tsar. This state duma lasted until 1912 and was known as the duma of lords and lackeys. A fourth state duma was elected in November 1912 and lasted until the outbreak of the First World War, when it was suspended by the tsar.

Although not a radical institution, the state duma did introduce some important reforms. The land captains, introduced during the reign of Alexander III, were replaced by justices of the peace. Workers received health and accident insurance for the first time and a plan was introduced to established primary education for all within 10 years. This plan was never implemented because of the First World War.

In addition, the government made strident attempts to eradicate radical opposition to the regime. Tens of thousands were arrested and faced imprisonment or internal exile in Siberia and thousands were hanged. Although it was ruthless, the repression brought back law and order. Political assassination dropped dramatically by 1908–09.

Pyotr Stolypin

The politician most closely associated with restoring law and order to Russia following the 1905 Revolution was **Pyotr Stolypin.** He joined the Council of Ministers in April 1906 and became chairman by July 1906, the equivalent of prime minister. From 1906 until his own assassination in 1911, Stolypin became the major influence on government policy. He was the person most responsible for the brutal repression following the revolution.

However, Stolypin knew that to avoid another revolution, he had to reduce the social and economic problems facing Russia that were held to be the prime responsibility for the 1905 Revolution. From 1906 to 1911, Stolypin introduced a number of important reforms with which he hoped to modernise Russian society and at the same time preserve tsarism. In November 1906, he introduced a law that freed peasants from control by their commune; this allowed them to move freely around Russia. In the same month he proposed the creation of a peasant land bank which would offer peasants loans. Finally on 1 January 1907, he abolished the redemption payments that peasants were still paying following the Emancipation of the Serf decree of 1861. The combined effect of these reforms cannot be underestimated. Stolypin had freed the vast majority of Russia's rural population to move freely and to acquire finance to develop their plots of land. In 1905, only 20% of peasants owned their land, by 1915 this had risen to 50%. These changes were reflected in increased agricultural yields. By the outbreak of war in August 1914, Russia was on the verge of a major period of modernisation. Unfortunately, the war greatly disrupted this process.

The impact of the First World War

The First World War had a profound impact on Russia. During the war, Russian forces suffered massive casualties and by February 1917, the country faced a major political, military and economic crisis that resulted in the fall of the tsar.

Regardless of Russia's stability on the eve of war, the period 1912–14 seemed to resemble the years immediately before the 1905 Revolution. In 1912, in the Lena Goldfields, in Siberia, a strike and demonstration led to the deaths of several strikers at the hands of the authorities. The Lena Goldfields Massacre sparked off a wave of industrial unrest across Russia in the succeeding 2 years. In June 1914, Moscow faced a general strike. In a way, the outbreak of the First World War had a stabilising effect on Russian society. The war against Germany and Austria-Hungary in defence of Serbia had a galvanising effect on Russia. The country was affected by a national wave of patriotic enthusiasm. Thousands cheered the army as it marched to the front to defend 'Mother Russia'. The only political group which opposed the war was the Social Democrats; in particular, the Bolsheviks led by Lenin. However, Lenin was in exile and Social Democrat activity in Russia was constantly disrupted by the *Okhrana*. Yet by the winter of 1916, the situation had changed radically.

The military situation

The war began well for Russia; its armies invaded both Germany and Austria-Hungary. By early September 1914, just 5 weeks after the outbreak of war, Russian armies were in east Prussia in Germany and had overrun much of the Austro-Hungarian province of Galicia. Then disaster struck; in September, two Russian armies were heavily defeated by the Germans in the Battle of Tannenburg. In January 1915, the Russians were again defeated in the Battle of the Masurian Lakes and in early May, the Gorlice–Tarnow Offensive by both German and Austro-Hungarian armies recaptured Galicia and threw the Russians out of Poland by the end of the year. In 1915, an Anglo-French attempt to knock Ottoman Turkey out of the war and to supply Russia through the Black Sea failed in the Gallipoli campaign.

In the summer of 1916, the Russians attempted to win back the initiative with the Brusilov Offensive, which coincided with the entry of Romania on Russia's side. Initially successful, the Brusilov Offensive failed to make a breakthrough. Counter-attacks by German and Austro-Hungarian forces overran Romania and moved deep into western Russia. By the winter of 1916, Russia seemed to be on the brink of military defeat.

The Home Front

The outbreak of war in August 1914 brought together the Russian nation. The Union of *Zemstva* provided medical supplies for the army, while the Congress of

Representatives of Industry and Trade helped coordinate war production. By 1915, a central war industries committee had been created. In June 1915, the town dumas and *zemstva* joined together to form *Zemgor*, to aid war casualties. Even the tsar's daughters and members of the aristocracy volunteered as nurses.

However, the war had a traumatic effect on Russia; it was not prepared for a sustained European war where war production was one of the keys to success. From the beginning of the war, the Baltic and Black Seas were closed to Russian shipping, bringing to a virtual end any foreign trade and supplies from Russia's allies, Britain and France. As the war progressed, the German and Austro-Hungarian armies captured some of the best agricultural land in Russia; they also disrupted the Russian railway network. These developments led to food shortages in cities such as **Petrograd** and Moscow, which became acute in the winter of 1916–17.

The cost of fighting a major modern European war was enormous. The government budget rose eightfold between 1913 and 1916. To pay for the war, the government merely printed more money, which fuelled inflation. The cost of living rose 200% between 1914 and 1916. With a reduction in the food supply to cities becoming increasingly serious, by Christmas 1916 the government was facing a domestic crisis.

To make matters worse, the government was poorly led. At the beginning of the war, **Tsar Nicholas II** was the head of government but he lacked the organisational skills and leadership associated with his two predecessors. He was described by contemporaries as weak and ineffective. In September 1915, the tsar made a fateful decision. He decided to take personal command of the Russian Army at the Front, replacing his uncle Grand Duke Michael. From September 1915, the tsar was held personally responsible for Russian reverses at the Front and for the army's large casualty figures.

In Nicholas' absence the control of the government passed to his wife, the Tsarina Alexandra. The tsarina had virtually no experience of government matters. She was also German and rumours abounded that she was sympathetic to the enemy. In addition, she relied heavily on the advice of a Siberian Orthodox mystic, **Gregori Rasputin.** He had been at the royal court since 1907, when his supposed mystic powers temporarily helped to halt the medical condition afflicting her son, the **Tsarevich Alexis**, who suffered from **haemophilia**. Following the tsar's departure to the Front, it was rumoured that Rasputin had undue influence over the tsarina. The poor state of the Home Front was blamed directly on their joint role in government.

By the winter of 1916, plots to overthrow the tsar began to develop. These did not come from opponents of the tsarist regime but from its supporters, who believed nothing short of the removal of Nicholas II and his wife Alexandra could save monarchic rule in Russia. One aspect of the plotting was to murder Rasputin — a decision taken by the Russian aristocrat, Prince Felix Yusupov. Rasputin was allegedly poisoned at a dinner in his honour. As the only witnesses were Yupusov and his friends, they put forward the story that Rasputin survived absorbing enough poison to kill four men. Then he was shot and finally his body was thrown into a hole in the frozen

River Neva. These stories only helped exaggerate the legend of Rasputin and his malign influence over Russian government. Unfortunately, once Rasputin was dead, he could no longer be held as the scapegoat for the shortcomings of Russian government.

The February Revolution, 1917

In many ways the outbreak of revolution in Russia in February 1917 resembled the outbreak of the 1905 Revolution. Both began with demonstrations and both were spontaneous; the difference came in the result. The 1917 February Revolution led to the abdication of Tsar Nicholas II and his son Alexis on 2 March. From that date, Russia was technically a republic but this was not proclaimed officially until the summer. The February Revolution brought to an end 300 years of Romanov rule and helped change Russia forever.

The February Revolution began on 9 January 1917 with a strike and subsequent demonstration by approximately 140,000 workers in Petrograd. Their main grievances were food shortages and high food prices. On 14 February, another strike took place in Petrograd by approximately 100,000, concerned with the high cost of living and poor working conditions. Neither strike nor demonstration was broken up by the authorities. The government then made matters worse by announcing that bread rationing would begin on 1 March.

A major event on the road to revolution came on 23 February. To commemorate International Women's Day, thousands took to the streets of Petrograd. This coincided with a major strike at the Putilov Engineering works. On the following day, workers' committees or soviets began to be formed across Petrograd to articulate workers' demands.

On 25 February, the turning point of the revolution occurred. Over 200,000 demonstrators took to the streets of Petrograd. However, when asked to fire on the demonstrators, the troops refused to obey orders. Although troops did fire on demonstrators the following day, killing 40, this was the first sign that government authority in the capital was breaking down. On 27 February, military units across Petrograd refused to obey orders and sided with the demonstrators.

In an attempt to maintain power, on the 14 February, the government recalled the state duma. Since its disbandment in August 1914, a group of deputies had continued to meet as a **Progressive Bloc**. By 27 February, the government was beginning to lose its nerve and attempted to dissolve the state duma. However, instead of dissolving the duma, it formed a 12-man committee. This committee proclaimed itself the Provisional Government of Russia.

Throughout the development of these events the tsar was at Russian army headquarters (*Stavka*) at Mogilev. He attempted to win back power by offering to share power with the Provisional Government on 28 February, but it refused. The tsar attempted to get back to Petrograd by train on 1 March. He got as far as Pskov (180 miles from Petrograd), where his train was halted by railwaymen sympathetic to the Provisional Government. In a railway siding, on 2 March, his train was visited by members of the Provisional Government who asked him to abdicate. He did so without demur, also abdicating on behalf of the heir apparent, Tsarevich Alexis. It was widely felt that Alexis' haemophilia meant he would be too sick to take on the role of tsar. An attempt was made the following day, 3 March, to save the Romanov dynasty, when the tsar's brother Michael was offered the throne, but he refused.

The 300-year Romanov dynasty seemed to end abruptly and accidentally. No one planned the February Revolution but disillusionment with the tsar's rule, the military disasters at the Front and the increasingly dire living conditions in the cities helped create the climate for revolution. In addition, the majority of revolutionary events occurred in and around the capital, Petrograd. These helped shape the revolution that the rest of the country followed.

Glossary

haemophilia: an inherited blood disorder which prevents the blood from clotting. Even the slightest bruise can lead to internal bleeding and, ultimately, death.

Petrograd: name given to St Petersburg following the outbreak of the First World War.

Progressive Bloc: a group of deputies formed in the summer of 1915 from members of the Kadet, Octobrist and nationalist factions within the state duma. They formed a majority in the state duma and wanted the tsar to issue a programme of political reforms that would win public support for the tsarist regime.

Key figures

Tsarevich Alexis (1904–18): the only son of Tsar Nicholas II and Tsarina Alexandra. A sickly child from birth, he was diagnosed with haemophilia. From 1907, the Russian monk, Gregori Rasputin allegedly used hypnotic techniques to control the effect of the disorder. It was widely believed Alexis would not survive into adulthood. On the orders of Lenin, he was murdered by Bolsheviks, along with his entire family, in July 1918.

Nicholas II (1868–1918): the last tsar of Russia, he succeeded his father in 1894. He married a German aristocrat, Alexandra, who tended to dominate him. He lacked his father's strength of character and found the problems facing him as tsar daunting. He mismanaged internal affairs and can be held ultimately responsible for the outbreak of the Russo–Japanese War and 1905 Revolution. Following Witte's advice, he published the October Manifesto.

In July 1914, he made the fateful decision to mobilise the Russian Army in the July Crisis, which led to a war with Germany and Austria-Hungary. He also made what proved to be a disastrous decision in September 1915 to take personal command of the Russian Army. As a result, he was away from Petrograd when the February Revolution broke out. His decision to abdicate for himself and his son Alexis effectively brought to an end 300 years of Romanov rule in Russia. Nicholas II and his family were placed under house arrest after the revolution. When the Bolsheviks came to power, the family was moved to Ekaterinburg in western Siberia, where in July 1918, on the orders of Lenin, they were all murdered.

Gregori Rasputin: a Siberian 'holy man' who had known the Russian royal family since 1905. His influence over the royal family, and, in particular Tsarina Alexandra, developed from 1907. Rumours abounded in the capital that he was a drunk and sexually promiscuous. It was even suggested that he had a sexual affair with the tsarina. Following the tsar's decision to become commander-in-chief in September 1915, Rasputin was accused of influencing the tsarina's control over the Russian government. In December 1916, he was murdered by members of the Russian aristocracy, in the hope that his removal would revive the Russian war effort and improve government.

Pytor Stolypin (1862–1911): born in Dresden, Germany, of Russian parents. He became chairman of the Council of Ministers — the Russian equivalent of prime minister — from 1906 until his assassination by a political extremist in 1911. He led the tsarist government in attempts to restore law and order following the 1905 Revolution. His brutal repression restored order but resulted in hundreds of hangings and tens of thousands forced into imprisonment or internal exile. Faced with potential opposition from the state duma, he altered the electoral law to ensure a majority in support of the government. His economic reforms freed the Russian peasantry from redemption payments and subservience to commune control.

1917: the failure of the Provisional Government

Political and economic problems

The Provisional Government was based on a self-appointed committee comprising former members of the fourth state duma (1912–14). The majority of members were from the two Liberal parties, the Octobrists and the Kadets. The only person representing the workers or peasants was a lawyer, **Alexander Kerensky**. The head of government was Prince Lvov, a member of the Kadet Party. The Provisional Government filled a political vacuum vacated by Tsar Nicholas II. As a result, it lacked the political credibility of being elected directly by the Russian people.

It also faced a major problem of authority from another quarter. During the February Revolution, workers' committees were created and these sent representatives to a Petrograd soviet. The Petrograd soviet sent representatives to a nationwide body representing committees of workers, peasants and soldiers, the All-Russia Soviet. Like the Provisional Government, the All-Russia Soviet claimed to represent the will of the Russian people. Both organisations issued laws and directives. The most famous directive from the All-Russia Soviet was Order Number 1, which required all army officers to be elected by their men. The Provisional Government lacked the authority to countermand this directive. Order Number 1 had a detrimental effect on the army as it undermined officer authority. Officers who wished to take the battle to the enemy were usually deselected.

The Provisional Government also inherited the social and economic crisis that did so much to bring down the tsar. Cities and towns were still short of food and in the countryside, law and order began to break down with the collapse of the tsarist regime. Peasants began seizing land and anarchy reigned across Russia.

In the midst of this chaos, the Provisional Government had to contend with continued fighting in the First World War. When the tsar fell from power, the Allies were concerned that Russia might pull out of the war. Enormous pressure was placed on the Provisional Government to continue fighting. The majority of the Provisional Government now viewed the war as one between democracy and German militarism and supported the war effort. The Russians were pressured into beginning an offensive against the German and Austro-Hungarian armies. In June 1917, the Russians launched an offensive but after a brief initial success, the Russian army began first to retreat and then to disintegrate.

Disillusionment with the war caused a political crisis which forced Prince Lvov from power in July 1917. He was replaced by the radical Alexander Kerensky, who headed a more left-wing government. However, Kerensky continued fighting the war with a promise that the Allies would provide loans for Russia following an Allied victory. By doing so, Kerensky further undermined the authority of the Provisional Government. Across Russia demands began to appear for an end to the war. Such demands were fuelled by radicals, who began returning to Russia following the overthrow of the tsar. The most important exile to return was Vladimir Lenin, leader of the Bolsheviks.

The impact of Lenin's return to Russia

Lenin was in Zurich, Switzerland, when the February Revolution occurred. For much of the period 1900–17, Lenin was in exile across Europe. For a brief period during the 1905 Revolution he returned to Russia. Lenin spent much of his time in exile developing his own political ideas and creating first a faction and then a political party that was under his personal control.

An important event during Lenin's time in exile was the Second Party Congress of the Russian Social Democrat Party. Initially, this met in Brussels but due to police harassment, it moved to London. At this congress Lenin helped establish his Bolshevik faction of the party through his insistence that the Social Democrats should comprise only committed revolutionaries. This caused a split with other Social Democrats, who became known as Mensheviks. In 1912, the Bolsheviks decided to become a separate political party.

Lenin's ideas

Lenin was a Socialist who followed the ideas of the German thinker, Karl Marx. He believed that capitalist-style societies would eventually be overthrown by industrial workers, who would create a just and equal society. However, Russia was a society where approximately 80% of the population consisted of peasants engaged in agriculture. Even in 1917, industrial workers comprised less than 3% of the population. Lenin's response to this situation was to suggest that the Bolshevik Party would lead a revolution that would ultimately create a Socialist society. However, even within his own Bolshevik Party, many believed that Russia had to go through a phase of government under the Liberal-dominated Provisional Government before a Socialist revolution could succeed.

An immediate problem facing Lenin in Zurich was how to get back to Russia to foment Socialist revolution. Fortunately for him, the Germans were willing to allow Lenin and his followers to travel across Germany to neutral Sweden and then on to Petrograd via Russian-occupied Finland. The Germans saw Lenin as a potential ally, as he had frequently denounced Russian participation in the First World War. If Lenin could help remove Russia from the war, the Germans would then be able to concentrate their armed forces on the Western Front against Britain and France.

Lenin arrived at the Finland Station in Petrograd. He was met by a large enthusiastic crowd, which saw him as an exiled revolutionary who would support the Provisional Government. To almost everyone's surprise, he made a 90-minute speech atop an armoured car outside the station in which he denounced the Provisional Government. He demanded an immediate Socialist revolution.

April Theses

Lenin's ideas were put forward in more detail in what became known as the April Theses in a speech delivered on 3 April 1917. Lenin claimed that the February Revolution was a bourgeois revolution which gave power to the middle class. He believed that a socialist revolution, which would give political power to the workers, could take place immediately after the bourgeois revolution. This idea ran counter to the main principles of Socialist thought as put forward by Karl Marx and Russian Socialists like the Mensheviks. It also ran counter to the ideas of leading Bolsheviks such as **Zinoviev**, **Kamenev** and **Stalin**, who had all supported the Provisional Government before Lenin's return.

The aim of the April Theses was to win over his own Bolshevik Party, which he succeeded in doing. From April onwards, Lenin looked for opportunities to undermine the Provisional Government. The first opportunity took place in June, when Lenin attempted to use a demonstration against the Provisional Government to force himself into power; it was a complete failure.

The July Days

A major attempt to gain power occurred between 3 and 6 July 1917 and became known as the July Days. Support for the Provisional Government had fallen following the disastrous June Offensive, which saw mass desertions from the Russian Army. Street demonstrations occurred in Petrograd, encouraged by the Bolsheviks. Lenin hoped that he could use such demonstrations to bring down the Provisional Government in the same way that similar demonstrations had brought down the tsar in February but the whole plan backfired. The Provisional Government and the Executive Committee of the All-Russia Soviet met on the evening of 3 July and agreed to restore order. By 5 July, troops loyal to the Provisional Government returned to Petrograd from the Front to restore order. On the following day, the troops surrounded the Bolshevik headquarters and regained control. Lenin fled in disguise to Finland, believing that his planned takeover of power had gone forever. Yet within 3 months, the Bolsheviks were again in a position to make another bid for political power.

The Kornilov Affair

A key event in the change in Bolshevik fortunes was the Kornilov Affair at the end of August 1917. **Lavr Kornilov** was the commander-in-chief of the Russian Army in the late summer of 1917. Kornilov feared a left-wing plot by Bolsheviks and other extremists to take control of the Provisional Government. As a result, he decided to send troops from the Front to Petrograd in order to prevent a left-wing coup from taking place. The key figure in the Kornilov Affair was the prime minister, Alexander Kerensky. He panicked when he heard of Kornilov's decision to move troops to Petrograd. He feared a military attempt to overthrow the Provisional Government was in progress. He demanded Kornilov's dismissal and arrest; he also armed radical groups in Petrograd, including the Bolsheviks. The impact of Kerensky's action was to undermine his relations with the army. It also enhanced support for the Bolsheviks, who made propaganda from the threat of a right-wing military takeover.

All power to the soviets

Following the July Days, Lenin realised that his only chance of gaining political influence was through the All-Russia Soviet where Bolsheviks had a number of representatives. Lenin began a campaign demanding that all political power be handed to the soviets across Russia. This seemed a sensible strategy, as support for the Bolsheviks increased greatly following the Kornilov Affair.

Lenin supported the slogan of 'Peace, Bread, Land'. Under this slogan the Bolsheviks supported popular demands such as withdrawal from the First World War, more food for the cities and land for the peasants.

The Kornilov Affair and Lenin's new tactics on the soviets and new policies won increasing support for the Bolsheviks in cities such as Petrograd and Moscow. By October, the Bolsheviks were on the verge of gaining control over the All-Russia Soviet. For Lenin, this was the moment to strike for political power.

The Bolshevik Revolution of October 1917

Since 1917, historians and commentators have debated what actually took place. To some Western historians, the Bolshevik Revolution of October 1917 was a plot by a small, fanatical political party of the Left lacking popular support. To the Bolsheviks, the October Revolution was a popular uprising. A Soviet film called *October*, made in the 1920s, shows thousands of workers and soldiers storming the Winter Palace in Petrograd, the home of the Provisional Government. Which is the more accurate account of the October Revolution?

Lenin was the person who suggested an armed takeover of the government with soldiers and armed Red Guards. He was initially opposed by other leading Bolsheviks such as Kamenev and Zinoviev, but through force of personality and argument, Lenin got his way. To Lenin, the Provisional Government was on the verge of collapse; it lacked authority. Across the country peasants were seizing land and the Provisional Government lacked the power to stop them. Although still fighting in the First World War, the Russian Army was in no position to attack the German and Austro-Hungarian armies. In fact, the Germans began withdrawing troops from Russia in the early autumn to strengthen the Austro-Hungarian army on the Italian Front. In October 1917, these troops helped win a crushing victory that almost forced Italy out of the war.

Lenin also wanted to use the All-Russia Soviet as a cover for the Bolshevik seizure of power. He wanted to announce to the All-Russia Soviet at its meeting on 25 October that the Bolsheviks had taken power in its name. He was helped by an attempt of the Provisional Government to close down two Bolshevik newspapers for printing anti-government articles.

As a result, the Military Revolutionary Committee (MRC) of the All-Russia Soviet began planning for armed resistance against the Provisional Government. Fortunately for Lenin, the person who chaired the MRC was Leon Trotsky, who had joined the Bolshevik Party in July. Under the cover of the MRC, the Bolsheviks planned to occupy key installations across Petrograd. This took place on the evening of 24 October 1917. The signal for the start of the takeover was the firing of a blank artillery round from the cruiser *Aurora* that was anchored in the River Neva opposite the Winter Palace. Red Guards occupied the Winter Palace and captured most of the Provisional Government. The prime minister, Kerensky, escaped in a car. The Winter Palace had been defended by a women's detachment and some officer cadets.

On 25 October, Lenin announced to the All-Russia Soviet that the Provisional Government had been overthrown and the Bolsheviks were now in power in the name of the All-Russia Soviet. The 390 Bolshevik members of the Soviet supported the action. The Mensheviks had only 80 seats and the Social Revolutionaries possessed 180. Even here, the SRs were split, with the Left SRs supporting the Bolsheviks. As a result, the All-Russia Soviet endorsed the Bolshevik action.

The Bolsheviks were successful for a variety of reasons. Trotsky proved to be an effective organiser of the seizure of power. Throughout the October Revolution, Lenin stayed in the background, only returning to Petrograd in secret on 25 October, when he made the public announcement in the All-Russia Soviet. Lenin's decision to support 'Peace, Bread, Land' won Bolshevik support across Russia and Lenin's timing of the takeover was crucial. The Provisional Government had lost virtually all authority by the end of October. Russia was in a state of chaos and anarchy. Rumours abounded about which political group might take over; Lenin ensured it was the Bolsheviks.

Key figures

Lev Kamenev (1883–1936): a moderate Bolshevik who at first supported the February Revolution before Lenin's return and opposed the Bolshevik seizure of power in October 1917. He was a leading member of the Politburo, 1917–24. He was chairperson of the Moscow Soviet, 1918–24. He sided with Zinoviev and Stalin against Trotsky following Lenin's death. He was dismissed from office by Stalin in 1925 and was accused of anti-Soviet activities in 1936, which led to his execution.

Alexander Kerensky (1881–1970): born in Simbirsk, the same town as Lenin. A socialist lawyer who became a member of the first Provisional Government in March 1917 as minister of justice. He became prime minister in July 1917 and was overthrown in the Bolshevik seizure of power in October 1917. He fled into exile and died in New York.

Lavr Kornilov (1870–1918): had Cossack origins and fought with distinction in both the Russo–Japanese and First World Wars. In 1917, the Provisional Government appointed him commander of the Petrograd garrison. Following his dismissal by Kerensky and the Bolshevik seizure of power, Kornilov joined the Whites in the Civil War; he was killed in action in 1918.

Josef Stalin (1879–1953): born Josef Dzugashivilli in Georgia, he adopted a variety of nicknames such as Koba, but became universally known as Stalin with the Bolshevik faction by 1905. He was in Siberia when the February Revolution occurred. He supported the February Revolution until Lenin's return in April 1917 and played a minor role in the Bolshevik seizure of power. He was commissar for nationalities in Lenin's first government. From 1917 to 1924 he amassed considerable political power as commissar of the Workers' Inspectorate, from 1919 he was the link member between the Politburo and Orgburo and from 1922 he was first general secretary of the Communist Party. He succeeded Lenin as party leader and head of government. He ruled the USSR with great brutality until his death in March 1953.

Gregori Zinoviev (1883–1936): born Gershon Radomyslsky; like other leading Bolsheviks he adopted an alternative name. He joined Lenin in exile in 1903 and during his career, he was for a time editor of *Pravda* and the first head of Comintern. He sided with Kamenev and Stalin against Trotsky following Lenin's death. He was dismissed from office by Stalin in 1927 and in 1936 put on trial and executed for alleged anti-Soviet activities.

1917–24: Lenin in power

Problems facing Lenin in October 1917

Taking power in Russia during October 1917 was easy compared to holding on to it. Lenin faced enormous problems, which had to be overcome if the Bolsheviks were to stay in power. First, Lenin had to form a government; he did so by going into coalition with the Left SRs. He also had to implement promises made by the Bolsheviks. In his first months in office, the All-Russia Soviet, now acting as the Russian national parliament, passed a series of decrees; a decree set up a new style of government. At the top was the Council of People's Commissars, known as **Sovnarkom**. Lenin was to be chairperson, the equivalent of prime minister. The Decree on Land confiscated all private landownership and placed land in the hands of the peasants. In many ways the Bolsheviks were accepting what had already happened. Finally, a Peace Decree declared that Russia wished to withdraw from the war and put forward the idea of an immediate ceasefire or armistice.

The Treaty of Brest-Litovsk, 1918

The decision to end the war was central to the survival of Lenin's new regime. The Germans and Austro-Hungarians were only too willing to have a ceasefire. In April 1917, the USA entered the war on the side of the Allies. With its huge economy and potential for employing a vast army, the USA's entry could turn the tide of the war in the Allies' favour. The armistice came into effect in December 1917 and negotiations for a peace treaty began at Brest-Litovsk (on the present day border between Poland and Belarus). Negotiations began on 22 December, with Alfred Joffe and Leon Trotsky as the main negotiators for the Bolsheviks. Lenin stayed in Petrograd as head of the government. The Bolsheviks took the opportunity to hand out anti-war leaflets to German soldiers at Brest-Litovsk, much to the annoyance of the German negotiators.

Unfortunately for the Bolsheviks, the Germans and Austro-Hungarians demanded extremely harsh terms for a treaty. They stipulated that the Bolsheviks give up control of the Baltic states of Estonia, Latvia and Lithuania. They also had to relinquish control of Poland, large parts of present-day Belarus and the whole of Ukraine. These areas contained about half of Russia's industry and best agricultural land. So severe were these terms, that Trotsky broke off negotiations. He declared that Russia was in a position of neither peace nor war. This did not impress the Germans, who continued to advance into Russia and threatened to occupy Petrograd.

On Lenin's insistence, the Bolsheviks returned to the conference table and in March 1918, peace treaties were signed with Germany and Austria-Hungary (the Treaties of Brest-Litovsk and Bucharest). Although the terms were harsh, Lenin knew that in order to survive in power, the Bolsheviks had to end the war. The terms offered at Brest-Litovsk caused intense debate within the Bolshevik Party and almost split it wide open. It also caused a split with Lenin's coalition partners, the Left SRs, who began plotting their own overthrow of Lenin's government.

Consolidation of power

Although Lenin created *Sovnarkom* and dominated the All-Russia Soviet, he still had serious political problems. Before its fall from power, the Provisional Government had proposed elections to a Constituent Assembly, whose task would be to draw up a new constitution for Russia. Lenin felt his position was too vulnerable to cancel these elections so they took place as planned on 12 November 1917. In the election the Bolsheviks won 25% of the vote; the largest party was the SRs, with 40% of the vote.

On 5 January 1918, the Constituent Assembly met for its one and only time. Lenin demanded that the Constituent Assembly should be subservient to the decrees passed by *Sovnarkom*. When the Constituent Assembly refused, the Left SRs and Bolsheviks left and under the command of Trotsky, Red Guards dispersed all the other delegates. Trotsky claimed the Constituent Assembly had been discarded and placed in the dustbin of history. From that moment, it was clear that the Bolsheviks did not represent the majority of the Russian population. To continue in power, the Bolsheviks, who in 1918 had renamed themselves Communists, had to resort to political repression and terror. In response, anti-Bolshevik forces began to resist Lenin's rule. It was the beginning of a bloody civil war that was to last 3 years and result in millions of deaths.

Civil War, 1918–21

The most serious problem facing Lenin during his period of rule was the Civil War. Those historians who saw the Bolshevik seizure of power as a takeover by a small but committed revolutionary party realised that such an event was inevitable. The Civil War contained a number of separate conflicts.

First, in 1918 and 1919, Allied countries such as Britain, France, Japan and the USA sent troops to Russia in a bid to keep Russia in the First World War. As the Bolsheviks opposed continuation, they came into conflict with Allied forces of intervention. British forces were located around the White Sea in north Russia near the port of Archangel. Japanese forces occupied the Pacific seaport of Vladivostok. However, once the First World War came to an end, these forces were gradually withdrawn.

During 1918, the Bolsheviks faced the Czech Legion. These were former troops of the Austro-Hungarian Army of Czech and Slovak origin who had been captured by the Russians. After the Bolshevik Revolution, they left their prison camps in Siberia and made their way along the Trans-Siberian Railway westward in a bid to get involved in the First World War. Numbering approximately 40,000 strong, these troops came into conflict with the Bolsheviks but, like the Allied forces, they left Russia at the end of the war.

In 1918, the Bolsheviks also had to contend with the German and Austro-Hungarian armies. On 8 July, the German ambassador to Russia, von Mirbach, was assassinated by a Left SR in Moscow. As a result, German and Austro-Hungarian troops marched further into Russia and threatened to overthrow Lenin's government. Fortunately for Lenin, the Germans and Austro-Hungarians had to divert troops to the Western and Italian Fronts respectively in August 1918.

content guidance

With the collapse of central political authority during 1917–18, many of the ethnic groups that made up the Russian empire began to declare their independence. Finland declared its independence at the end of 1917, followed by the Baltic states. Nationalist groups also attempted to create a separate and independent Ukraine, Armenia and Georgia. Bolsheviks and native Communists were engaged in fighting in all these areas. The conflict in Ukraine was made more complicated by the existence of a Green Army under **Nestor Makhno**. He was an anarchist who, at various times during the Civil War, fought with and against the Bolsheviks for his own ends.

After the signing of the Treaty of Brest-Litovsk and the establishment of a dictatorial regime under Lenin, the Left SRs became disillusioned with the Bolshevik-controlled government. In July 1918, they attempted their own takeover of power. Several leading Bolsheviks were assassinated and Lenin narrowly escaped death at the hands of an assassin in Moscow. The Bolshevik-controlled armed forces and secret police put down the uprising with severity.

The most serious opponents to the Bolsheviks in the Civil War were the Whites. These were mainly supporters of the tsarist regime but they also included individuals who were simply anti-Bolshevik. Supplied by the Allies and containing members of the old tsarist army, the Whites posed a serious military threat. They set up their own governments. In Siberia a separate government was formed under **Admiral Kolchak. General Deniken** controlled large areas of southern Russia, while **General Yudenich** controlled a White Army close to Petrograd. In 1918, it looked as if it was only a matter of time before the Bolsheviks were defeated but against the odds, Lenin was triumphant.

The Bolsheviks were successful for a variety of reasons. First, they were well led and had a clear sense of purpose: survival. For instance, the royal family was under arrest by the Bolsheviks in the west Siberian town of Ekaterinburg, However, when it looked as if they might be freed by White forces, Lenin ordered the entire family to be assassinated. Under Lenin's effective and ruthless leadership, the Bolsheviks also ensured that their armies were adequately supplied. The Bolsheviks were greatly assisted by Leon Trotsky who, as minister of war, created the Red Army and led the Bolsheviks to victory, directing military operations from an armoured train. Trotsky even used former tsarist officers to fight, holding their families hostage as an incentive.

The Bolsheviks controlled the heartland of European Russia in the area from Petrograd to Moscow to Tsaritsyn (now Volgograd and formerly Stalingrad). This area had the largest population and the Reds could transfer troops from one front to another with relative ease. Opponents of the Bolsheviks lacked unity and their attempts to win the Civil War were poorly coordinated. The Bolsheviks could defeat their opponents and in the course of 1919, they defeated Yudenich, Kolchak and Deniken. By 1920, only the White Army under General Wrangel in the Crimea remained but he was defeated by a large-scale Bolshevik offensive.

Not all Bolshevik actions in the Civil War were so successful. In 1920, in an attempt to spread Communist revolution westward, Lenin ordered the Red Army to invade Poland. The Red Army was heavily defeated on the outskirts of the Polish capital,

Warsaw. In the Treaty of Riga, that brought the Russo–Polish War to an end, Russia lost a large part of Belarus to the new Polish state. In March 1921, disillusionment with Bolshevik rule forced the sailors of the Revolutionary Baltic Fleet to mutiny at Petrograd's naval base at Kronstadt. Trotsky was given the task of subduing an uprising by a group which had been one of the most enthusiastic supporters of the Bolshevik Revolution of 1917.

Introducing communism, 1918–21

Comintern

When Lenin took power in October 1917, he planned to create a completely new state. Russia was to be the world's first Communist state, from which revolution would spread across the globe. Lenin saw Russia as capitalism's weakest link; he hoped, like all Communists, that his ideas would be accepted by other countries in the world. Communism was a world revolution, not just a Russian revolution. With this in mind, Lenin established the Third Communist International, or Comintern, in 1919. This was an international organisation of Communists from around the world. The Bolshevik Revolution had split Socialist parties in almost every country. The more extreme Socialists formed Communist parties and these new parties joined Comintern. Under the leadership of Gregori Zinoviev, Comintern planned to offer leadership and direction to the world Communist movement. However, within a short period of time, Comintern became an organ for Russian international policy. Lenin's attempt to 'export' the revolution also involved military means. The Russo–Polish War of 1920–21 was an attempt by Lenin to facilitate the spread of communism and it ended in complete failure.

State capitalism, 1917–18

Within Russia, Lenin attempted to move towards a Communist-style state almost immediately. In December 1917, he set up the Supreme Council of National Economy or *Vesenkha*. The aim of this organisation was to control the entire Russian economy from the centre. On 14 December, all Russian banks were taken over by the state and in the following month, Lenin refused to pay foreign countries any debts incurred by the tsarist and Provisional Governments.

In the first months of the regime, Lenin introduced an economic system which historians have termed 'state capitalism'. Workers took over their factories and began to run them, but without the knowledge and expertise of managers, these factories soon ran into difficulties. The amount of productivity dropped significantly as workers set their own hours of work and shortages of every kind occurred. To meet demand, a black market appeared; by June 1918, the Russian economy seemed on the verge of collapse. To make matters worse, Lenin faced the prospect of fighting a civil war — he had to act swiftly and ruthlessly.

War Communism

Lenin's response was the introduction of War Communism. As the name suggests, the whole economy was placed on a war footing. A Supreme Council was created to run the economy. All business enterprises were nationalised and put under strict government control. All private trade was banned as a way of destroying the black market. Strict rationing was introduced, with workers in essential industries receiving higher rations. Groups of elite workers were formed and were sent to factories to boost production when required. Those held responsible for not producing enough or accused of obstructing the war effort were arrested and sent to slave labour camps.

To ensure that the populations of cities were fed, squads of dedicated Communists were sent into the countryside to requisition corn from the peasants. Anyone caught resisting what was called the Urals-Siberian Method of Grain Procurement was either summarily shot or sent to a slave labour camp.

War Communism was fiercely resented by the majority of the population. Many workers complained that tsarist oppression had merely been replaced by Communist oppression. In the countryside, peasants either hid grain or just grew enough for their own needs. The result by 1921 was the outbreak of widespread famine across Russia, as the Communist squads merely took all the grain they could find.

War Communism also led to peasant uprisings; the most serious occurred in 1921 in Tambov Province. Large detachments of the Red Army had to be deployed to that province to restore law and order. In 1921, disillusionment with Communist economic and political policies led to the Kronstadt Uprising by members of the Revolutionary Baltic Fleet. By the spring of 1921, Russia seemed on the verge of economic collapse.

Lenin's response was to introduce a series of new policies at the Tenth Party Congress in March 1921. As the Red Army was fighting sailors of the Revolutionary Baltic Fleet, Lenin announced his New Economic Policy (NEP). Lenin claimed that War Communism had only been a temporary measure needed to win the Civil War. Now that the war was over, a new policy was required. Under the New Economic Policy, private enterprise was reintroduced, private markets reappeared and small private businesses were allowed. However, the government still controlled the major Russian industries which Lenin termed 'the commanding heights of the economy'. In the countryside, forcible requisitioning of grain was stopped. In its place peasants were allowed to keep all the grain they grew but they had to pay a tax to the government.

The New Economic Policy saved the Russian economy from collapse. By 1923, over 80% of businesses were again in private hands and grain production increased. However, the NEP also led to the rise of a new class in the economy, so called 'NEP men', who engaged in private trading and grew rich on its profits. To the more radical Communists, the NEP was a retrograde step, going backwards to capitalism, not forwards to the creation of a new Socialist society. Lenin tried to assuage their fears by claiming that the NEP was a temporary measure but he gave no indication of how long it would last. Lenin was a realist; he knew that to survive in power he had to give some independence to the peasants who comprised 80% of the population. In the last years of his rule, Russia was a nation of workers and peasants. The symbol of Communist Russia was the hammer and sickle, with the hammer representing industrial workers and the sickle representing the peasantry. It was up to Lenin's successor to bring about a truly Communist revolution within Russia.

Creating a Communist dictatorship by 1924

In October 1917, Lenin promised the Russian people a new society that was to be more fair and just than that under the Provisional Government or tsarist rule. Instead, he created a dictatorship that was more brutal, ruthless and wide-ranging than any that the tsars had introduced. Historians are split on why this occurred. Some Western historians believe that Lenin was always likely to create a dictatorship while others held that dictatorial rule was forced on Lenin by circumstance.

The Red Terror

The Bolsheviks had minority support in October 1917; in the November 1917 elections to the Constituent Assembly the Bolsheviks polled only 25% of the vote. How were they going to stay in power? It was not long after gaining power that Lenin came up with an answer: terror. In December 1917, he set up the All-Russia Extraordinary Commission for Combating Counter-Revolution and Sabotage, known as *Cheka*. This new organisation was a politically motivated terror police force under the direction of Felix Dzerzhinsky. The *Cheka* hunted down any person accused of being anti-Bolshevik. Thousands were tortured and subsequently murdered. Hundreds, if not thousands, were sent to slave labour camps known as the gulag. The *Cheka* was far more ruthless and brutal than the tsarist *Okhrana* — it ensured that the Bolsheviks would face no opposition. The *Cheka* suppressed the Left SR uprising of July 1918 and it continued to use terror tactics against any opponent of communism until it was replaced in February 1922 by the State Political Administration (GPU). At its height, *Cheka* had 260,000 members. The GPU merely carried on the tactics of *Cheka* under another name.

In March 1921, at the Tenth Party Congress, Lenin ensured that he had established a dictatorship when he convinced the Communist Party to accept the idea of democratic centralism. Lenin feared that the party might split over the introduction of the New Economic Policy, as had happened over the debate on the terms of the Treaty of Brest-Litovsk in 1918. Under democratic centralism, whatever decision was made by the ruling committee of the Communist Party, known as the **Politburo** had to be followed by all Communist Party members. This principle ensured that whatever policy Lenin decided in the Politburo would be accepted without discussion. By the time Lenin had his first stroke in 1922, he had established a regime that was a dictatorship more thorough than any experienced under the tsars.

By 1922, the Communists had won the Civil War and set to work creating a new political system for the multi-racial empire they had inherited from the tsars. In 1922, Lenin's government created the Union of Soviet Socialist Republics or USSR. This was a union of semi-independent republics; the largest, comprising 75% of the USSR, was the Russian Soviet Federative Socialist Republic (RSFSR). This covered what is approximately modern-day Russia. United with the RSFSR were the Ukrainian SSR, the Belorussian SSR and the Transcaucasian SSR. In time, other soviet Socialist republics were added. In central Asia, by the late 1920s, the Kazakh, Turkmen, Uzbek, Tajik and Kirgiz Soviet Socialist Republics were created. The Transcaucasian Republic was subsequently subdivided into Georgia, Armenian and Azerbaijan. Although technically self-governing, each SSR was governed by the Communist Party, which was answerable to Lenin's government in Moscow. The USSR gave the pretence of local government but it was in reality part of the Communist dictatorship.

Glossary

Politburo: the senior committee of the Communist Party that made all the important decisions between 1917 and 1924. During that time, the leading members of the Politburo were Lenin (chair), Kamenev (Moscow soviet boss and Lenin's deputy), Zinoviev (head of Comintern), Trotsky (head of the Red Army), Bukharin (editor of the Party newspaper, *Pravda*), Stalin (commissar for nationalities and general secretary) and Tomsky (trade unions).

Sovnarkom: the Communist name for the Committee of Ministers that formed the government.

Key figures

General Deniken (1872–1947): Anton Deniken fought in both the Russo–Japanese and First World Wars. He supported Kornilov's attempt to restore order in Petrograd in August 1917. After the Bolshevik seizure of power, he became the commander of White forces in southeast Russia. He was decisively defeated by Red forces at the battle of Orel in October 1919. After the Civil War, he went into exile in a variety of countries, ultimately settling in France. He died in New York in 1947.

Admiral Kolchak (1873–1920): Alexander Kolchak served in both the Russo–Japanese and First World Wars. He was the commander of White forces in Siberia and set up a White government, known as the Provisional All-Russian Government, based at Omsk in 1918. He was captured by the Czech Legion, which handed him over to the Red Army, who executed him.

Nestor Makhno (1888–1934): leader of the Revolutionary Insurrectionary Army of the Ukraine. As an anarchist, he opposed state authority, be it White or Red. He changed sides several times during the Civil War. At the end of 1920, following the defeat of Wrangel in the Crimea (the last White general), the Red Army attacked and defeated Makhno. He and his followers fled to Romania. He eventually went into exile in France, where he died.

General Yudenich (1862–1933): Nikolai Yudenich was commander of the Russian Army on the Caucasus Front in the First World War, where he led a successful campaign against the Ottoman Turkish army. He took command of White forces in northwest Russia in 1918 and led an unsuccessful attack on Petrograd in 1919. After the Civil War, he went into exile in France and Estonia.

Questions
&
Answers

This section contains five specimen exam questions. Two specimen answers are given to each question: an A-grade and a C-grade response. All the specimen answers are the subject of detailed examiner comments, preceded by the icon *e*. These should be studied carefully because they show how and why marks are awarded or lost.

When exam papers are marked, all answers are given a level of response and then a precise numerical mark. Answers are normally marked accordingly to five levels.

- **level 1**: 1–6 marks
- **level 2**: 7–12 marks
- **level 3**: 13–18 marks
- **level 4**: 19–24 marks
- **level 5**: 25–30 marks

Question 1

How far were the economic reforms of Witte the most important development within Russia between 1881 and 1903? (30 marks)

■ ■ ■

A-grade answer

The period 1881–1903 was a period of considerable change within Russia. As the most economically backward of Europe's five great powers, Russia entered a period of modernisation that began to transform the economy and society. The person most closely associated with this change was the minister of finance in the years 1893–1903, Sergei Witte. However, was Witte's 'Great Spurt' of economic modernisation the most important development within Russia in these years?

✐ The introduction is focused clearly on the question. It gives the historical context for subsequent discussion. The final sentence provides a clear link to balanced analysis.

Clearly Witte's economic reforms were of considerable importance. The centerpiece of his economic programme was the construction of the Trans-Siberian Railway. This enormous enterprise would link the cities of St Petersburg and Moscow with the great expanse of Siberia and eventually the Pacific Ocean at Vladivostok. The distance was 4,500 miles and it required enormous effort in terms of engineering. The cost of the construction was far beyond the domestic means of the Russian economy at the time. As a result, Witte was instrumental in acquiring foreign loans for Russia's economic development. Coming mainly from western and central Europe, Witte ensured that the construction was effectively financed. The construction of the railway helped open up the vast economic potential of Siberia and offer the first effective overland route to Russia's Pacific territories.

✐ This paragraph begins to deal directly with the assertion in the question. It makes an analytical statement in the first sentence and then backs this up with detailed supporting factual evidence. The final sentence makes an apt assessment.

Although the construction of the Trans-Siberian Railway was the centerpiece of Witte's economic reforms, it was not his only contribution to Russia's economic development. Witte ensured that the Russian government encouraged the development of capital goods as a way to stimulate economic growth. Under Witte's leadership, the Russian government encouraged the production of coal, iron and steel and oil. These were the building blocks of future economic growth. In the Donbass region of the eastern Ukraine, coal production increased markedly. So did the production of oil, which was centred on the Caspian Sea port of Baku. The impact of such reforms was impressive. Coal production almost tripled between 1890 and 1900, a position matched by oil production. By the time of his departure from office in 1903, as minister of finance, Witte had laid the foundations of future Russian economic growth.

However, the growth of the Russian economy cannot be seen as linked only to Witte. One of Witte's predecessors, Ivan Vyschnegradsky, in the 1880s, had begun the process of stimulating Russian economic growth through the acquisition of foreign loans.

ℓ The above paragraph provides an appropriate link to a balanced assessment of Witte's role.

Also, Witte may have been responsible for economic growth but he left unresolved major social and economic problems associated with the peasantry. Peasants still had to pay redemption payments and were under the authority of the village commune. In addition, Witte raised taxes on the peasantry to pay for economic growth, which caused deep resentment. Witte's reforms could not prevent the periodic outbreak of famine in Russia and his tax reforms helped fuel peasant uprisings, which occurred periodically throughout the 1890s and into the early years of the twentieth century. The rapid growth of urban industrial centres resulted in poor living and working conditions for industrial workers, who harboured resentment and grievances about their predicament. This helped fuel the outbreak of the 1905 Revolution. Although the Russian economy had grown markedly in the 1890s, Russia was still the most economically backward great power in the early years of the twentieth century.

It seems clear that Witte's reforms did bring considerable change but were they the most important development within Russia in the period 1881–1903? During this period, under Tsars Alexander III and Nicholas II, political repression was a significant aspect of Russian life. Many of the liberal reforms of Alexander II were reversed by his successors, Alexander III and Nicholas II. Russia became a police state, with the *Okhrana* arresting and imprisoning those who attempted to criticise the tsarist political system. The Statute on Measures to Preserve National Order and Public Peace, passed in 1881, meant Russia had the most oppressive political system and lack of civil rights of any of Europe's great powers. Part of this policy was the intensification of Russification, which made the Russian language the official language of government and education across the empire. Associated with this policy was the government-sponsored persecution of Jews. Ten of thousands of Jews were forced to leave their homes, many emigrating to the New World during the pogroms of the 1890s.

ℓ The two paragraphs above provide a balanced assessment of Witte's role. The first highlights limitations in Witte's policies. The second deals with other issues which might be considered more important for the period under discussion.

Therefore, Witte's economic reforms were an extremely important development. However, compared with the introduction of widespread political oppression under Alexander II and Nicholas II, perhaps it was not the most important development within Russia in the years 1881–1903.

ℓ **The answer is focused. It contains paragraphs that are linked to the question and to each other. A balanced assessment is offered and a clear conclusion reached.**

Level 5: 28/30

C-grade answer

Russia in the late nineteenth century was an economically backward country. Approximately 80% of the population were peasants working in agriculture. By the beginning of the First World War, Russia had experienced considerable economic change. A central person in the achievement of economic change was the minister of finance in the 1890s, Sergei Witte.

e There are clear links to the assertion in the question. However, the introduction is a little limited on historical context.

Sergei Witte was important in the development of Russia for a number of reasons. He realised that, unless Russia modernised economically, it might no longer be able to sustain its position as one of Europe's five great powers. By the late nineteenth century, economic power was increasingly the basis of military power. Witte realised that Russia had to exploit its economic potential to ensure it could rival Germany, Britain, France and Austria-Hungary militarily.

e This is an apt focus with an emphasis on the aims of Witte. However, it would have been better to concentrate on the consequences of his policies.

The most important project associated with Witte's period as finance minister was the construction of the Trans-Siberian Railway. This was to be the Russian equivalent of the transcontinental railroads that crossed the USA, linking the Atlantic with the Pacific Ocean. In the 1870s and 1880s, these railroads helped open up the economic potential in the American West. Witte's great plan was to achieve similar results in Russia's great untapped heartland of Siberia. This huge region had vast resources in terms of timber and metals. It could also be an area for the settlement of Russia's ever-expanding peasant population.

e This paragraph is relevant but requires more assessment of Witte's policies.

The project involved constructing a railway from the capital St Petersburg to the Pacific seaport of Vladivostok, a distance of 11,000 kms. The construction would involve tens of thousands of workers and would require large quantities of iron and steel. It would also act as a stimulus to the development of the engineering and construction industries within Russia. Finally, as a government-sponsored project, the construction of the Trans-Siberian Railway would bring great prestige to the Russian state and its ruler the tsar.

To achieve this great project Witte required finance. He found the money through encouraging foreign loans, as Russia lacked the ability to raise sufficient finance internally. In addition, he ensured that the Russian government would play a key role in developing the key industries of Russia — coal, oil and iron. Such intervention had important results for Russia's economic development. The production of these important areas of the economy tripled during Witte's period as finance minister. These developments laid the foundations for future economic growth in the twentieth century.

question

However, Witte's reforms were not all progressive. To help raise finance within Russia, he raised the taxes on the Russian peasantry. Peasants comprised 80% of the population, working in agriculture, with many living just above the poverty line. Witte's taxation, along with other developments such as population growth and periodic famines, led to a fall in the living conditions of this social group. By the time of Witte's departure from office in 1903, the Russian countryside was on the verge of major social unrest, which appeared during the 1905 Revolution.

The information contained in the paragraphs above is relevant but rather narrative-descriptive in format. It does contain assessment but this could have been more focused.

Therefore, Witte's economic reforms were of great significance within Russia in the period 1881–1903 and can be regarded as the most important development at that time.

The answer is relevant, contains some assessment but is unbalanced in its coverage. It does not discuss any other potential developments in the period 1881–1903.

Level 3: 16/30

Question 2

**To what extent was the lack of political reform the main cause of the
1905 Revolution?**   (30 marks)

■ ■ ■

A-grade answer

In January 1905, the demonstrations which resulted in Bloody Sunday sparked off the
1905 Revolution. The demonstrators were mainly factory workers who wanted the
tsar to assist in improving their poor living and working conditions. However, to
understand fully the reasons why the revolution took place and spread across Russia
during 1905, political issues have to be taken into consideration.

e The introduction is focused on the question and gives the historical context. It is also
linked to the assertion on the role of political issues.

In 1905, Russia was the most politically repressive of Europe's five great powers. All
political power was in the hands of the tsar, who appointed and dismissed all
government ministers and made law by decree. Russia lacked a national parliament.
Elections, where they did occur, were for small and rather limited local government
bodies known as *zemstva* in rural areas and dumas in towns. Political parties were
banned, the press censored and political dissent discouraged. As a result, the demand
for political reform was a major issue within Russia by 1905 and during the 1905
Revolution.

In 1905, virtually all the political parties and groups in Russia were linked to the
demand for political change. These groups covered a wide spectrum, from moderate
Liberals to social and political extremists such as the Social Revolutionaries and Social
Democrats. What all these groups had in common was a detestation of the repressive
and reactionary tsarist government.

It was clear that the importance of political reform during the 1905 Revolution must
be highlighted. The 1905 October Manifesto was an important development in the
defeat of revolution. It offered moderate political reform. This satisfied many of the
tsar's opponents, who now accepted this political change and ended their support for
the revolution.

e The first part of the answer deals directly with political issues, as required by the
question. Relevant supporting evidence is deployed to support assessment.

However, to see the causes of the 1905 Revolution purely in political terms is
simplistic. Many of the demands for political reform were linked with the desire for
a change in the social and economic position of much of the population. A major
cause of the 1905 Revolution was the social and economic crisis facing both towns
and countryside in Russia in the early years of the twentieth century.

2

question

Approximately 80% of Russia's population in 1905 were peasants who worked in agriculture. In the quarter century before 1905, Russia's peasant population increased rapidly, placing pressure on landholdings. In addition, peasants resented paying the redemption payments as part of the Emancipation of Serfs in 1861. Finally, peasants were subject to the authority of local communes, who had the power to redistribute peasant land and to limit peasant opportunities to move to cities. As a result, an important feature of the 1905 Revolution was peasant uprisings across European Russia. Although occasionally peasant demands were couched in political terms, the cause of their resentment was primarily social and economic.

Similarly, the rapid growth of Russian industry in the 1890s and early twentieth century led to a movement of population to the new industrial factories of towns like St Petersburg. These industrial workers lived in poor conditions and faced low wages and poor working conditions. A group of industrial workers were engaged in the demonstrations that led to Bloody Sunday. Their demands were essentially social and economic. However, many workers thought that their living and working conditions could not improve unless there was a change in the political system that had created them.

Events in the far east helped undermine respect for the government. In 1904, a war broke out between Russia and Japan. In 1904, Russia suffered humiliating military defeats at sea, at Port Arthur and on land, at the Battle of Mukden. Such reverses at the hands of a rising Asiatic power caused uproar in Russia and can be seen as a contributory factor in causing the 1905 Revolution.

The above paragraphs provide relevant evidence of factors other than those directly linked to political issues. However, even here an attempt is made to link various causes of the 1905 Revolution as part of an integrated assessment of the question.

Therefore, the lack of political reform was an important cause of the 1905 Revolution. The reactionary nature of the tsarist regime caused resentment across the political spectrum from Liberal to Socialist and Social Revolutionary. Demand for political reform was also linked directly to a widespread desire to alter the social and economic system within Russia.

The answer is focused, consistently analytical and supported by relevant factual evidence.

Level 5: 28/30

■ ■ ■

C-grade answer

On 22 January 1905, Father Gapon led thousands of demonstrators to the Winter Palace in St Petersburg. They came to get the support of the tsar for their demands for better living and working conditions. Instead of meeting the tsar, they were met by Cossack cavalry who attacked the demonstrators. The deaths of many of the demonstrators led directly to the outbreak of revolution across Russia.

✐ Although this opening paragraph is linked to the issue in the question the link is implied and not explicit. It is rather too narrative in format.

The events of Bloody Sunday sparked off widespread strikes and demonstrations across Russia. These outbreaks of unrest plagued Russia throughout 1905. The causes of these demonstrations were mainly social and economic. However, the demonstrators did also call for political reform.

Another set of social and economic problems helped create the conditions for the 1905 Revolution. The Russian peasantry was experiencing major problems by 1905. They had to pay high taxes to help pay for Russia's economic development. Many also had to pay redemption payments associated with the abolition of serfdom. They also faced periodic famines due to poor harvests. The combined resentment of the peasants helped spark off spontaneous peasant uprisings, known as *jacqueries*. Peasants attacked landlords and destroyed landlords' property. As a result, these outbreaks had little to do with a desire for political reform.

In October 1905, the tsar issued the October Manifesto. This manifesto promised political reform. It promised the creation of an elected national parliament. It also promised an increase in individual rights such as press freedom and freedom of religion. The October Manifesto was supported by many Liberals, who saw it as an important concession by the tsar. The October Manifesto was an important reason why the 1905 Revolution failed, so it suggests that desire for some political reform had been a cause of the revolution. Even so, many political groups were still disappointed with the October Manifesto and kept up their opposition to the tsar's government. These included Social Democrats and Social Revolutionaries. Some of these groups were involved in an uprising in Moscow in December 1905. Others helped form the St Petersburg Soviet, which demanded political reform.

✐ Relevant material is deployed but analysis appears within a narrative-descriptive framework.

In conclusion, the desire for political reform was an important cause of the 1905 Revolution. However, it was not the only cause. Far more important was the social and economic crisis facing Russia.

✐ **The answer is relevant but limited in both balance and depth. It also contains some narrative section where analysis is implied.**

Level 3: 18/30

TO39351

Question 3

How far was the weakness of the Provisional Government the main cause of the successful Bolshevik seizure of power in October 1917? (30 marks)

■ ■ ■

A-grade answer

In early March 1917, Nicholas II abdicated as tsar of Russia. It was the final episode in the February Revolution, which saw the end of over 300 years of Romanov rule. The Provisional Government inaugurated a new era of democratic rule which was widely supported across Russia. However, within 8 months, the Provisional Government was overthrown. Was the short-lived Provisional Government the cause of its own downfall or were other factors more important?

ℓ The introduction sets the issue in its historical context. The final sentence offers a clear link to possible balanced analysis.

To an extent, the weakness of the Provisional Government was the cause of its own downfall. The February Revolution was an unplanned, spontaneous overthrow of the tsarist government. In the political vacuum created by the tsar's fall, the Provisional Government took power. It was not directly elected by the Russian people but comprised former deputies of the Fourth Duma. Part of the Provisional Government's legitimacy was its proclamation that it would hold elections to a Constituent Assembly that would draw up a new democratic constitution for Russia. However, due to circumstances, the elections for the Constituent Assembly were not planned until mid-November 1917 and this delay was a factor that undermined the Provisional Government's authority.

The Provisional Government had to share political power with the All-Russia Soviet of workers', peasants' and soldiers' deputies. This body had spontaneously developed during the course of the February Revolution and also claimed a right to govern Russia. It issued its own decrees which helped undermine the authority of the Provisional Government. One of the most notorious Soviet decrees was Order Number 1, which declared that all officers in the Russian Army had to be elected by their soldiers. This undermined the authority of the officers and had disastrous consequences in the June Offensive of 1917.

ℓ The above paragraphs provide a clear link to the question. They begin with analytical statements supported by detailed evidence.

Another factor which undermined the Provisional Government's authority was the narrow political base of its membership. Most of the first Provisional Government of February–July 1917 came from the Liberal parties, which received support from only a small minority of the Russian population. Peasants and industrial workers had only one representative, the Socialist lawyer, Alexander Kerensky. Even after July 1917, the second Provisional Government did not offer a representative cross-section of Russian society. As a result, political groups such as the Social Revolutionaries and Bolsheviks were excluded from the Provisional Government and, instead, looked to the All-Russia Soviet for representation.

A significant factor in the short term of the Provisional Government was the decision to continue fighting in the First World War. By early 1917, the war had already cost Russia millions of casualties and was very unpopular. In June 1917, the Provisional Government launched an offensive against the forces of the Central Powers on the Eastern Front. The failure of that offensive undermined the faltering authority of the Provisional Government. From June 1917, army discipline began to collapse. By October 1917, the Provisional Government had limited authority mainly centred on the capital, Petrograd.

Another self-inflicted factor which helped destroy the Provisional Government was the Kornilov Affair of August 1917. Kerensky's actions in demanding the arrest of Kornilov and his arming of radical groups such as the Bolsheviks paved the way for the Bolshevik seizure of power in October 1917. By that time, the main fear of revolution came from the right of Russian politics.

✐ The answer sustains a clear analytical focus with links between paragraphs.

However, in assessing the success of the Bolshevik seizure of power, credit must be given to the Bolshevik leaders such as Lenin and Trotsky. Lenin developed the strategy in the middle of 1917, to demand all power to the soviets, because he realised that it was through local soviets and the All-Russia Soviet that the Bolsheviks could gain political power. Lenin also devised the popular slogan of 'Peace, Bread, Land'. The Bolsheviks won support across Russia for advocating an end to Russia's participation in the First World War, an end to food shortages and land for the peasants.

Trotsky was important in his role in the All-Russia Soviet as head of the Military Revolutionary Committee. Under the guise of that committee, Trotsky carefully planned the Bolshevik takeover of power at the end of October 1917. Although Lenin supported the idea of an armed takeover, it was Trotsky who executed that plan.

✐ These paragraphs highlight other factors in Bolshevik success.

By October 1917, the Provisional Government had lost virtually all authority. The army was disintegrating, peasants were seizing their own land across Russia and people in the towns and cities were demanding food and a lower cost of living. It was widely believed that a political group would overthrow the Provisional Government. Thanks to Lenin's foresight, that group would be the Bolsheviks.

✐ **A balanced, analytical account which contains clear analysis that is sustained throughout the answer.**

Level 5: 30/30

■ ■ ■

C-grade answer

In February 1917, the Provisional Government replaced the tsar's government as rulers of Russia. However, the Provisional Government did not last long; by the end of October 1917 it was overthrown by Lenin and the Bolsheviks.

e This is a short and rather general introduction.

The Provisional Government was made up of former members of the Fourth Duma. This group had formed a committee to negotiate with the tsar and ask for his abdication in February and March 1917. The Provisional Government that took over power in March 1917 was made up of Liberals, with Alexander Kerensky — a Socialist — as the only representative of the working class. In its period in power it had to face a wide variety of problems which, in the end, led to its downfall.

One of the most serous problems facing the Provisional Government was Russia's involvement in the First World War. The Allied powers were keen on Russia remaining in the war as it forced Germany to fight a two-front war. The Provisional Government badly needed loans from the Allies so it was forced to continue fighting. In June 1917, the Provisional Government launched an offensive on the Eastern Front in support of the Allied war effort. Unfortunately, the offensive failed and this led directly to the eventual collapse of the Russian Army. By October 1917, the desire for peace was widespread throughout Russia. So the Provisional Government's decision to continue in the First World War was an important reason why it collapsed.

Another reason was the fact that it had to share power with the All-Russia Soviet. The Soviet represented workers and peasants. Like the Provisional Government, the All-Russia soviet thought it had the authority to pass laws. So from March to October 1917, Russia was faced with two potential governments. The Provisional Government, as its name suggests, was to hold power for a short period of time until a directly elected government could take power. Therefore, the dual power and need for a permanent government meant its rule was to be short-lived.

e The above paragraphs offer a clear link to reasons associated with the short lifespan of the Provisional Government.

The Provisional Government was faced with other problems. Central authority began to break down. Peasants began seizing land and the power of the Provisional Government was limited because the armed forces began to fall apart and workers tended to follow the lead of the All-Russia Soviet rather than the Provisional Government.

By October 1917, the Provisional Government had lost much of its authority. It had split political power with the Soviet and its decision to continue fighting in the First World War undermined its authority, which helps explain why it was so short lived.

e **This is a valid focus on the question but it is rather one-sided. It does not address important issues such as the role of the Kornilov Affair and the role of Lenin and the Bolsheviks.**

Level 4: 19/30 marks

Question 4

How far was the Bolshevik victory in the Russian Civil War due to the leadership of Lenin and Trotsky? (30 marks)

■ ■ ■

A-grade answer

When Lenin and the Bolsheviks seized power in October 1917, they did so by taking over from a weak Provisional Government. Taking political power was easy compared to holding on to power from October 1917. The biggest challenge to Bolshevik rule was the Civil War of 1918–21. Bolshevik victory ensured the continuance in power of the world's first Communist state. There were a wide variety of factors behind the Bolshevik victory and clearly one of these was the leadership of Lenin and Trotsky

🖉 The question is placed in a clear historical context and the leadership roles of Lenin and Trotsky are highlighted in the final sentence.

Lenin's political leadership was central to Bolshevik success. As the founder of the Bolshevik Party, Lenin had enormous personal authority. It was Lenin's decision to oppose the Provisional Government and it was Lenin who suggested that the Bolsheviks seize power in October 1917. Lenin was able to keep the Bolshevik Party united. He was also ruthless in dealing with political opponents. Lenin set up *Cheka* in December 1917 to root out political opposition. As a terror police force, *Cheka* was far more ruthless and effective than the tsarist *Okhrana*. By instituting the Red Terror, Lenin ensured Bolsheviks had control over their own area.

Lenin was also effective in dealing with potential threats to his leadership outside the Bolshevik Party. In July 1918, when White forces were closing in on Ekaterinburg it was Lenin who ordered the murder of the entire Russian royal family. Lenin was determined that the royal family should not fall into White hands and become a figurehead for opposition to the Bolsheviks.

An important aspect of Bolshevik victory was the introduction of War Communism in 1918. Lenin ensured that war production was maintained and the towns and cities fed by the adoption of ruthless tactics. Groups of committed workers were used to maintain war production and reduce bottlenecks in production when they appeared. Through the use of the Urals-Siberian method of grain procurement, Lenin used Bolshevik supporters to take grain forcibly from the peasants to feed the cities. However, Lenin was pragmatic enough to see the need for change when problems arose. Following the Tambov peasant uprising and Kronstadt naval mutiny, both in early 1921, Lenin abandoned War Communism and replaced it with the New Economic Policy to ensure that the Bolsheviks would stay in power in the latter stages of the Civil War.

e The above paragraphs offer a detailed assessment of Lenin's role in winning the Civil War, including both economic and political issues. Analytical statements are supported by detailed factual evidence.

Like Lenin, Trotsky's leadership was also a major factor in explaining Bolshevik victory in the Civil War. Trotsky founded the Red Army and organised the military side of the Bolshevik war effort. Trotsky went from front to front in his armoured train, organising Bolshevik military forces. Trotsky also used former tsarist officers to lead detachments of the Red Army. Under Trotsky's leadership, the size of the Red Army grew to almost 5 million by 1921. Red Army cavalry units played a critical role in the Bolshevik victory and it was Trotsky's strategy that led to military success.

e This paragraph deals directly with Trotsky's leadership. However, it could mention Trotsky's important role as a member of the Politburo.

However, although very important to Bolshevik success, the leadership of Lenin and Trotsky was just one set of factors ensuring victory. The Bolsheviks also faced a divided and poorly organised enemy in the form of the Whites. Generals Deniken, Yudenich and Admiral Kolchak failed to coordinate their military forces, allowing the Bolsheviks to confront them individually.

Another reason was that anti-Bolshevik forces lacked the unity of purpose possessed by Lenin and his party. Anti-Bolshevik forces contained those who wished to see the return of a tsarist-style regime to Liberals, Socialists and Social Revolutionaries. Such disunity was an important factor in explaining Lenin's success.

Finally, Bolshevik success can be explained by the control the Bolsheviks had over central European Russia. They controlled the area between Petrograd, Moscow and Tsaritsyn. This gave the Bolsheviks a clear advantage over their foes, because their area contained a large population and Red Army troops could move easily from front to front, instead of operating on the periphery of the Russian state.

e The above paragraphs offer a balanced view by highlighting and assessing other factors that could explain Bolshevik victory.

Therefore, the leadership of Lenin and Trotsky was central to explaining the success of the Bolsheviks in the Civil War. However, they were not the only reasons in explaining Bolshevik success.

e **The answer offers balanced focus and deals with both Lenin and Trotsky. It balances their role with other factors in explaining Bolshevik success. Analysis is supported throughout with relevant evidence.**

Level 5: 26/30 marks

■ ■ ■

C-grade answer

Between 1918 and 1921, the Bolsheviks had to fight a bitter civil war. Bolshevik victory in that war ensured the survival of Lenin's regime, the first Communist state in the world.

⟳ This is a general introduction with limited links to the assertion in the question.

The Bolsheviks won for a variety of reasons. One was the weakness of their opponents. In 1918 and 1919, the Bolsheviks had to face armies sent by the Allied powers such as Britain, France and the USA, as a bid to keep Russia in the First World War. Once the war was over, these forces were withdrawn.

Another set of opponents that the Bolsheviks faced were the Czech Legion, which comprised former prisoners of war from the Austro-Hungarian army. The Czech Legion posed a major threat to the Bolsheviks in Siberia in 1918 and early 1919. However, again, once the First World War was over, the Czech Legion returned home to the newly created state of Czechoslovakia.

Other forces against the Bolsheviks lacked organisation and coordination. The White forces had occupied Siberia, southern Russia and northwest Russia near Estonia in 1918 and 1919. Under different and competing White generals, the Whites lacked the organisation to defeat the Bolsheviks. The Reds were able to meet the threat from each White army separately

Opponents of the Bolsheviks were divided in their political beliefs. Some were nationalists, like the Finns and the Poles. Others wanted a return to a type of tsarist state. Others wanted major social and economic change. The only thing they had in common was their opposition to the Bolsheviks.

⟳ The above paragraphs offers reasons to explain Bolshevik victory but the answer highlights factors other than those identified in the question.

In contrast, the Bolsheviks were well led by Lenin and Trotsky. Lenin led the Bolshevik government while Trotsky organised and led the Red Army. Between them, they offered effective leadership, which their opponents lacked.

⟳ This is a short paragraph and, although relevant, is lacking in supporting evidence.

Therefore, a major reason why the Bolsheviks won the Civil War was the leadership of Lenin and Trotsky. However, the Bolsheviks also won because of the lack of unity and purpose of their foes.

⟳ **The answer is relevant but unbalanced. The section dealing with Lenin and Trotsky is lacking in depth.**

Level 3: 16/30 marks

Question 5

To what extent had Lenin created a Socialist society in Russia by the time of his death in 1924?

(30 marks)

■ ■ ■

A-grade answer

When Lenin took power in October 1917, he planned to create a completely new type of state and society: the world's first Communist regime. During his time in power, Lenin introduced many major, far-reaching reforms that transformed Russia, but were these reforms sufficient to create a Socialist society?

🖉 This is a relevant and focused introduction. The final sentence opens up the opportunity for balanced assessment in the succeeding paragraphs.

In 1918, the Bolsheviks established workers' control in factories, known as state capitalism. Unfortunately, this change increased worker control but led to a major fall in production and had to be abandoned in favour of War Communism. As the name suggests, War Communism was introduced to meet the demands imposed on Lenin's regime by the need to win the Civil War. State control over the entire production process and the abolition of private business and trade suggests that War Communism was a major move in favour of a Socialist society. However, the strict and ruthless control over the economy caused resentment. This was most closely seen in the treatment of the peasantry. Using forcible grain requisitioning, the Bolsheviks were able to feed the population in the towns and cities they controlled. However, this was done at a cost. Peasant resentment turned into open rebellion, as in Tambov Province in 1920–21. It also led to a major reduction in the planting of grain by the peasants, leading to widespread famine by 1921.

🖉 This is a focused paragraph, assesing the role of War Communism.

In order to save the regime from collapse and the country from economic devastation, Lenin abandoned War Communism in March 1921 and replaced it with the New Economic Policy. The NEP introduced private business and private trade. It also abandoned forcible grain requisitioning. Although Lenin's regime maintained control over major industry, the commanding heights of the economy, this was a major retreat from a truly Socialist society. Therefore, by the time of his death in 1924, Lenin had moved partly towards creating a Socialist-style economy but had abandoned a full-blown Socialist model in March 1921.

🖉 This paragraph is linked to the previous paragraphs and assesses the consequences of Lenin's economic policies.

When Lenin took power in October 1917, he did so as the leader of the workers and poor peasants of Russia. Instead of introducing representative government, Lenin introduced the Red Terror and Communist dictatorship. The Constituent Assembly was forced to close after only 1 day, in January 1918. Russia was ruled by a small clique of leading Bolsheviks from the Politburo. The press was severely censored, as all aspects of the media came under Bolshevik control and became organs of propaganda for the Bolshevik regime.

A key feature of Lenin's rule was the recreation of a terror police force. The Provisional Government had abolished the *Okhrana*. Instead, Lenin created the *Cheka*. As a ruthless force of approximately 250,000, the *Cheka* hunted down political opponents of the Bolsheviks. Tens of thousands were imprisoned without trial. The *Cheka* also ran the gulag, a nationwide network of concentration camps filled with opponents of the regime. By the time of his death, Lenin had created a dictatorship far more ruthless than the tsarist regime he had condemned. In many ways, Lenin was merely a Red tsar.

🖉 The above paragraphs focus on the consequences of Lenin's policies and provide an assessment of Lenin's political policies.

Therefore, by 1924, the Russian economy had many of the features of a Socialist society. The state controlled large sectors of the economy. Yet over 75% of the Russian population were still peasants working their own land. Instead of a truly Socialist society, Lenin had created a state of workers and peasants. The society created by Lenin was far from free and open. It was a ruthless dictatorship, where only the views of Lenin and the Bolsheviks were accepted. This was shown clearly in the Kronstadt uprising of March 1921, when the revolutionary Baltic Fleet sailors openly rebelled against Lenin, accusing him of abandoning socialism.

🖉 **The candidate gives a balanced analysis that identifies a range of policies and assesses their consequence in relation to the assertion in the question.**

Level 5: 27/30 marks

■ ■ ■

C-grade answer

Between 1917 and 1924, Lenin ruled Russia and introduced a wide variety of reform that helped transform Russian society.

🖉 This is a rather limited and undeveloped introduction requiring greater focus on the issues raised in the question.

Between 1918 and 1924, Lenin introduced a variety of economic reforms that led to a great increase in the state control of the economy. Between 1918 and 1921, Lenin introduced War Communism. This policy led to direct state control over the entire economy as a means of winning the Civil War. All private trade and business was banned and Lenin used violence and force to achieve his aims. For instance, grain was forcibly taken from the peasantry to feed the cities. In spite of its unpopularity, it could be argued that War Communism did move Russia towards a Socialist-style society.

question

However, at the Tenth Party Congress of March 1921, Lenin abandoned War Communism and replaced it with the New Economic Policy. This new policy allowed the existence of private trade and small privately-owned businesses. Lenin even admitted this was a retreat from socialism. However, he said it was a price the regime had to pay in order to prevent a complete economic collapse.

The information in the above paragraphs is relevant but it is used in a narrative descriptive way, with only implicit analysis of the question.

Lenin also introduced a political dictatorship which seemed far from his political ideals. The Bolsheviks banned all other political parties. From March 1921, they even banned dissent in their own party, with a ban on factions. The Bolsheviks also abolished parliamentary style elections. Lenin ruled Russia as a dictator. Even though unpopular, Lenin was able to stay in power through the use of terror and violence. He used the *Cheka* police to deal with political foes and anyone else accused of being an 'enemy of the state'.

This is a relevant paragraph but it lacks depth.

Therefore, by the time of his death, Lenin had moved some way towards creating a Socialist society but in doing so, he also created a dictatorship.

This is a relevant answer but some information is used descriptively. There is also a lack of balance, with limited coverage of the consequences is of Lenin's political policies.

Level 3: 15/30 marks